D1651918

DAM BREAK IN GEORGIA

Sorrow and Joy at Toccoa Falls

K. NEILL FOSTER

with **ERIC MILLS**

© 1978, Horizon House Publishers
© 2000 Toccoa Falls College
© 2017 Toccoa Falls College
All Rights Reserved

Dam Break in Georgia
ISBN 978-1-885729-17-0

Toccoa Falls College
Toccoa Falls, GA 30598
(706) 886-6831
www.tfc.edu

To our bereaved brothers and sisters
Who were willing to open
Still-fresh wounds
To tell this gripping story
To us—and to the world

CONTENTS

FOREWORD

When You Pass Through The Waters

Tragedies, like the one that happened in the early morning hours on November 6, 1977, are difficult to discuss. They are even harder to write about.

So many lives were lost. To be exact, 39 members of our college family were swept away with flood waters when an earthen dam above the Toccoa Falls College campus gave way and sent an estimated 176 million gallons of water rushing down a narrow ravine toward the area where many of the faculty, staff, and students lived and lay sleeping.

The immediate impact of the flood appeared devastating; and certainly, it would have been except that God had another plan. News accounts of the tragedy quickly spread around the world, but so did the testimonies of faith from those who had survived the flood.

Adversity Is An Inescapable Part Of Life

If we live long enough each one of us will experience it. The sudden death of a spouse, the loss of a job, or the betrayal of a loved one can leave us feeling hopeless and defeated, but we are not. We have immeasurable hope though Jesus Christ. He offers us beauty for ashes—a garment of praise instead of despair (Isaiah 61).

For several months before the flood Aunt Mary Williams

had gathered a group of friends to pray "hard" for the college because she sensed something big was going to happen. One wonders how she must have felt knowing that God had allowed her to have such insight. However, instead of turning to thoughts of fear and doubt, she turned to prayer and placed her trust in an omnipotent God, whom she knew could not fail.

Mary Williams and husband Paul had been students at the college in the 1920s. Back then it was known as Toccoa Falls Institute. Like so many before and after them, they met at the school and fell in love. But when graduation came, Paul moved back to Texas to help with the family's farm, and Mary went to Cuba as a missionary. Within a year, however, they were both back at Toccoa Falls saying their marriage vows and beginning a life together that would take them back to Texas and eventually back to Toccoa Falls in 1947.

When the Williams returned to the school, Paul became the supervisor of the dairy and Mary became the head of Christian Service. They were known simply as Aunt Mary and Uncle Paul to the campus family. Over the years, they had seen many changes at Toccoa Falls College. The school had grown from a small, mountain institute into a four-year college with alumni serving the Lord around the world.

Mary did not perceive "something big" as meaning something horrendous. She wasn't geared to think or pray that way. But she was sure that whatever was coming would change the course of the college's history and bring a new sense of hope to her beloved school.

It did, but none of us would have recognized its coming. If we had, we certainly would have beseeched God to change the course of history, if possible, in order to spare the lives of those we knew and loved. Just days before the flood, Paul Williams had admired the work he had completed on a small bridge that crossed the Toccoa Creek and connected the lower campus to the area where many of the married students lived.

"It is so strong," Paul said with a twinkle in his eye, "it will be able to go through a flood." Several days later, Paul's bridge was put to the test. It survived, but neither he nor his beloved wife Mary did.

When Adversity Strikes

What do you do when adversity strikes? How do you handle the suddenness of such loss and heartache?

One of the first things we need to do is recall the promises of God: "Do not fear," is God's Word to His children from the book of Isaiah, "for I have redeemed you; I have called you by name; you are mine! When you pass through the waters, I will be with you; and through the rivers, they will not overflow you. When you walk through the fire, you will not be scorched, nor will the flame burn you. For I am the Lord your God . . . " (43:1-3).

Secondly we must remember that God is not the author of evil. We live in a fallen world and until Christ returns for us, we will experience heartache and tragedy. However, we can take solace in the fact that He is the only One who can take evil and turn it around for His glory and our good.

Prayer is key to overcoming feelings of fear, doubt, and confusion. It is in times of prayer we confess our dependence on the Lord and seek His strength and wisdom for each crisis.

- When we are helpless, He is able
- When we are inadequate, His grace is sufficient
- When we cry out to Him, He hears our prayers and responds with faithfulness
- When we are overcome with doubt, fear, or sorrow, God is our refuge and infinite source of comfort and hope.

I believe the Toccoa Falls College family was changed in an eternal way the night of the flood. Many of the students admitted that they had drifted in their devotion to Christ and began to wonder if they could make the necessary commitment to do God's work.

Adversity has a way of refining and refocusing us on the goal God has set before us. Satan had hoped that this tragedy would mean the defeat of many of God's servants and particularly the end of Toccoa Falls College.

What he received was a mighty, resounding *No!* as hundreds in the Toccoa Falls community recommitted their lives to Christ and eventually thousands around the world responded with the same commitment because of the faith and determination of this amazing college community.

Graduation took place as scheduled in May 1978, and to this day Toccoa Falls College continues to do what God first directed Dr. and Mrs. Forrest to do in 1907— through Christ-centered education, developing godly character in men and women for service in His kingdom.

The Way Ahead

Just as God has a plan for Toccoa Falls College, He has one for our lives. As with the exiles to Babylon in Jeremiah's time, He has a plan for us: "'I know the plans that I have for you,' declares the Lord, 'plans for welfare and not for calamity to give you a future and a hope.'"

How do we handle adversity when it comes? Try beginning where Mary Williams began—with prayer:

- Acknowledge your sense of helplessness before the Lord. Immediately before the flood, prayer flowed from the college community, and spread around the world. When you pray, God hears your cry and is moved to respond according to your need and His will for your life.
- Acknowledge God's ability and not your own. Nothing stirs the heart of God like faith expressed through prayer. By

confessing your inability and acknowledging His ability, you essentially place your trust in Him and declare your dependence on Him.

- Acknowledge His intimate care for His children. Even now, we are encouraged by the personal accounts and testimonies of those who courageously went through this horrendous tragedy. Today, there is little physical evidence of what happened early that November morning, but what does remain is the faith and testimony of those who lost dear family and friends.

- Acknowledge that adversity is a tool in God's hand. Often heartache, disappointment, and sorrow are the very instruments that God uses to polish us for His likeness. Therefore, when trouble comes, you can be sure that the Lord is at work in your life—allowing your faith to be tested and your endurance strengthened for even greater service.

Maybe you are facing a deep sorrow and you feel as though the floodwaters have climbed so high that you will not be able to continue. *Do not give up.* God is faithful, and He will heal your brokenness and give you a fresh sense of hope and strength.

A LETTER OF INTRODUCTION

THE WHITE HOUSE

WASHINGTON

March 14, 1978

Dear Friends,

This is a story about faith. It is a story that will affect
every person who has ever doubted, for this is a personal
testimony that there is inherent courage within us to face
the challenges of life and death.

I visited Toccoa Falls College on the day after the disaster
that you will read about in this book. I went because I hoped
that I could comfort those who had survived. Instead I was
enveloped by hope and courage and love.

The miracle of Toccoa Falls confirms what I believe. God
loves us and will help us always. He gives us unlimited
strength when we trust in him.

This is a story that will never have an ending.

Sincerely,

Rosalynn Carter

I. FLOOD OVER THE FALLS

CHAPTER 1

DADDY, DON'T LET ME GO

Barbara Eby literally leaped out of bed just before the water came.

"The dam's broken!" she shouted, not even knowing how she knew.

Dave Eby, her husband and the Dean of Men at Toccoa Falls College, was sleepy and incredulous. "You're crazy!" he said. "Get back in bed." Then he heard sounds that brought him instantly to a full alert.

Barbara hurried to the bedroom where their three small children, Kimberly, Kevin, and Kelly, were asleep. As she headed down the hall, she noticed that the nightlight was still on in the bathroom. Almost simultaneously, she saw it go off and heard the rushing water.

Just that week she had moved all three children into one room to make available another room in which they could play. She headed first for Kimberly, 7, and carried her to where Dave was in the master bedroom.

As Barb headed back for Kevin, 5, and Kelly, 3, Dave tried to bash out a window in the bedroom. As he smashed the glass and the frame, blood poured from his arm. But he still wasn't through to the outside. Beyond the glass there was plastic which he could not penetrate—the water was already up to that level. Punching the plastic, Dave says, was like punching Jell-O.

Suddenly a torrent of water burst through the plastic. The powerful current swept Dave and Kimberly out of the bedroom and slammed them into the utility room. Eventually it washed them right out of the house.

Meanwhile, Barb had problems of her own.

When she reached the children's bedroom, she swept the other two children into her arms. One in each arm, she stepped into the hallway. Just as she did so, more water poured in and she heard Dave shout, "Hold on, we're going!"

The water was coming rapidly now, but she braced herself in the hallway and managed to keep her footing. She waded through the water to a room divider just past the end of the corridor. By the time she reached it the water was to her chest.

She could hear Dave and Kimberly struggling in the utility room and wanted to join them, but then the refrigerator tipped, blocking the door.

Barbara knew she and the children had to stay above the water. The divider, a solid structure about chest-high, seemed to be the answer. And reaching up from that divider were three decorative wooden spindles.

She told the children to hold on to her tightly while she attempted to climb onto the divider's level counter. As she struggled, she got all wrapped up in her long nightgown, but she somehow got her knee on the counter and rose to her feet, then climbed part way up one spindle, the children desperately clinging to her all the while.

From there she shouted, "David! David!" But there was no answer. She told Kevin that Daddy and Kimberly were dead, and that just the three of them were left. Her young son began to pray earnestly.

Household furniture was banging around Barbara and the children now, but the divider served to shield them from it. Then the spindles ripped loose from the ceiling, fell over about a foot, and little Kelly almost slipped from Barbara's grasp into the swirling water.

But somehow Barbara held on to her, though for how long she could continue to do so she didn't know. Her arm felt weak and numb, and she told Kevin, who was at the top of the spindle, that he would simply have to hang on for himself. If she was going to keep Kelly's head from going underwater, she would need both her hands.

Though he had been washed from the house, Dave Eby had somehow managed to retain his hold on Kimberly. He recalls feeling shingles in the water outside and clambering onto the roof of his home. Kimberly was still holding on.

Dave says the sound on the rooftop was like the roar of a jet taking off. Sitting there on the peak, both father and daughter felt sure that the rest of the family had been lost.

Dave was worried about the trees that the flood was tossing around like toothpicks. Some were two feet in diameter, and he feared that one of them would topple onto the roof of the house.

From his vantage point David saw a partition about five feet wide floating near the creek bank—which was only about ten feet from the house—so he decided to put his little girl on his back and jump. Had he been a swimmer he might have jumped beside the partition instead of on it. But when his feet struck the partition it shattered and little Kimberly lost her grip on her daddy and disappeared into the current. Dave went down, too.

Dave recalls, "I thought it was the end, and I knew if I took another breath I'd be in heaven. But I thought I'd better not—it would be suicide! Coming back up I bumped into the house, and then I felt two small arms wrap themselves around my neck and heard my little girl giggle, 'Daddy, don't let me go again!' She was laughing."

Dave had surfaced by the front door of his battered home. From there, with his head above water and Kimberly on his back, he could shout to his wife and children inside.

He grabbed the frame of the screen door and pulled himself inside. Straddling the screen door, with the water up to his chest, he heard his young wife say from the spindle, "I'm too tired, I can't make it."

They prayed earnestly then. Dave said he shouted at God—he really wanted Him to hear!

Incredibly, and much to their relief, the water fell about two feet.

The crisis had passed. The family was safe. Barbara inched down to where she could touch the floor once again. Then she lowered the children to the solid counter. David looked for a way out of the house to safety.

Soon, over destruction and debris, the Eby family clambered up the rocky cliff against which their floating house had lodged. Since they had all survived they could not believe that anyone else had died.

The dam had burst. The worst natural disaster in the state of Georgia since 1939 had already hungrily devoured little children and devastated sleeping families.

Nearly six percent of the college community had been wiped out in one cruel stroke. Most of the damage, at any given place, occurred in about twenty seconds.

November 6, 1977, was barely an hour and thirty minutes old.

This story does not begin, of course, with the sounds of the Toccoa Falls College flood. The roar of several freight trains, fierce and terrible in the narrow valley, was but one description of the thunderous noise surrounding a sad drama that became more painful—and triumphant—as events unfolded.

The voice of the Lord is over the waters; the God of glory thunders, the Lord thunders over the mighty waters.

PSALM 29:3

CHAPTER 2

HE FINGERED HIS TEN DOLLAR BILL

"I surely appreciate your kindness, sir. The price is certainly reasonable. Only . . . "

"Only what?" barked the older man.

"It's about the terms, sir." Mr. Forrest reached into his pocket and fingered his ten dollar bill.

"What about the terms? I haven't even mentioned them yet."

"I know—but I have only ten dollars, and no tangible place to get any more."

Today Toccoa Falls College is situated just outside the city of Toccoa, 100 miles northeast of Atlanta and seven miles from the border of South Carolina.

Situated on 1,100 acres of choice property between the Great Smoky Mountains and the Piedmont, Toccoa Falls College is strikingly beautiful. On college-owned property is located Toccoa Falls, a 186-foot cataract that plunges into a gorge-like box canyon. Toccoa Creek then meanders through the campus, under the concrete bridge at Georgia's Route 17, and eventually empties into Lake Hartwell, one of the largest man-made lakes in the United States.

Toccoa Falls College was begun by Dr. R. A. Forrest in a rather dramatic way. Forrest had only ten dollars in his pocket—and nowhere to get more. Undaunted, he approached a banker in Toccoa. The man owned a very desirable piece of property; and Forrest knew he would want money, a sizable down payment, and good terms. And he had a right to ask them. But young Forrest wanted something, too. So he breathed a silent prayer, wet his lips, and stammered, "How much do you want for the hotel?"

"Twenty-five thousand dollars is a fair price, it seems to me. That will include the hotel and about one hundred acres surrounding it."

"Will Toccoa Falls be on that hundred acres?"

"Yes, sir. There's a little piece of land that won't be included, though. My power plant is built there; and I'll retain that small piece of property and the water rights to Toccoa Creek above the Falls."

"Fair enough, sir," replied Mr. Forrest. "But tell me, what about our lights here?"

"Oh, we'll furnish you light with no obligation as long as there's water to turn the generator."

At that point, Forrest, with just ten dollars to back him up, made his rather daring offer.

As the businessman drew his breath and opened his mouth, the young minister watched, fascinated yet fearful. Suddenly R. A. Forrest's words tumbled out.

"Sir, I know this must sound presumptuous to you, a businessman and a banker. But I know God wants us to establish a school for Him here. Sir, I'll pay you ten dollars (I have only that and my return ticket to Atlanta), and the Lord and I will owe you the other $24,990 on the $25,000 deal if you'll trust the Lord and us."

"I can trust the Lord," was the dry response. The businessman held out his hand for the ten dollar bill.

And so it was that the beautiful property on a placid creek

was purchased in 1911.[1] It was that same gurgling stream which became, that fateful morning of November 6, 1977, a howling monster of incredible brutality and power.

About one-half mile back from the lip of Toccoa Falls stood Kelly Barnes Dam, a structure originally built in 1897 of red Georgia earth. The lake was later enlarged and the new earthen dam was finished in 1948. Behind the dam was Kelly Barnes Lake, fifty-five acres of placid, fish-filled water. The lake contained 700,000 tons of water, 176 million gallons; and from the air it was one of the most scenic lakes in Georgia. The bottom of the lake, since it was man-made, contained some vegetation and the tall stumps of some trees that had remained over the passing of time.

The Army Corps of Engineers stated that after the dam broke, the waters at the top of Toccoa Falls had developed a terrible velocity. In the half mile between the dam and the lip of the escarpment, Toccoa Creek drops 600 feet. The falls itself is 186 feet high.

The water may have come over the falls at 150 miles per hour. It could have had a velocity of 120 miles per hour as it exploded out of the canyon. Certainly, as it slammed into Morrison Hall, an empty dormitory that stood in its path, only solid rock could have withstood it. Hydrologists on the scene would say only that the water could have been going between 50 to 150 miles per hour.

Prior to the disaster, college personnel periodically inspected the dam. In fact, just hours before it broke, two volunteer firemen, Chief David Fledderjohann and his aide Ron Ginther, ascended the slippery road and observed the level of the lake. Water seemed to be emerging into Toccoa Creek in the usual manner. The surface of the lake was several feet below the top of the dam and the secondary spillway for excess water was not in use.

There was, however, some concern about the dam. Observation, even, of its condition—but no apparent cause for alarm.

Below, directly in the path of the pent-up water, lay a sleeping campus.

As nearly as can be guessed, at approximately 1:25 a.m. the pressure of the water behind Kelly Barnes Dam somehow became irresistible. Unseen by human eye, the powerful water tore at the earthen dike. Tiredly—tragically—it gave up.

And suddenly all the fury of death itself was surging down the slope toward the lip of Toccoa Falls.

Dave Eby, Dean of Men at the college, says he sensed two distinct things—first, a vibration and then a thud. This may have been the first rush of boulders and debris over the falls. A student heard a sound like the puncturing of a balloon.

The water plunged over Toccoa Falls, a cataract thirty feet higher than Niagara. In those awful moments, the morning of November 6, it really was Niagara.

There was a turbine-like effect. The falls and box canyon created a perfect tunnel and, for split seconds at least, the canyon held all the pent-up violence. But almost instantly the gorge was full and at its narrow mouth the water spewed out in all its horror and fury. The action was similar to that of a fire hose. The mud, uprooted trees, falling boulders, and roaring water—all were vomited out of the canyon.

As the waters boiled out of the gorge, a power pole bearing a transformer toppled and electric lines were tossed into the river where they snarled and snapped like high-voltage whips. The effect was such that one of the men staying in Forrest Hall, the men's dormitory, compared it to the Fourth of July.

Massive geysers surged skyward as the water slammed into obstacles in the narrow valley. Debris was tossed as high as sixty-five feet above the surface of the creek under normal conditions. Cars were twirling and smashing into each other.

Another immediate result was that for the second time that evening, the lights went out on the college campus. They also went out in the residences in the path of the flood and in Trailerville, a cluster of mobile homes occupied by married students and their families. The darkness compounded the fury of the flood.

Gate Cottage, the first college building to feel the force of the waters, stood just west of the canyon's mouth. Curiously, the building survived. Its stone-front walls may help explain why, but the main reason for its survival is that it stood just outside of the way of the main rush of water. Even so, the current of water collapsed doors and windows and bumped pieces of furniture around before flowing on through. Strangely, some of the glasses in the restaurant at Gate Cottage remained on the shelves, and some of the dishes remained intact in their cabinets. And a roll of paper towels was wet only part way through. Had the dam burst eleven hours later, perhaps sixty people would have been dining there in the restaurant, one of the finest in the area.

In seconds, the water reached the Bandy residence. Dr. Julian Bandy was a former president of the college (seventeen years) and also served nine years as vice president of The Christian and Missionary Alliance, the religious society with which the independent college is associated. Bandy's administration was one of development, consolidation, and building; and it was under his leadership that many of the structures soon to disappear were built.

Dr. Bandy was off preaching at Naples, Florida, at the time, but his 24-year-old grandson, Greg, was still at home. Hearing the roar of the water, he looked out of the window. All he saw was water. Though his window was perhaps thirty feet above the level of the creek, he couldn't even see Forrest Hall, the four-story dormitory across the narrow valley. He was the first human witness of the flood.

Possibly, the darkness hindered observation. Perhaps the power failure made the dorm invisible. But just possibly the rush of water of the canyon and the hose-like effect had actually created a hump of water. If it really was moving at over 100 miles per hour at that point, the water had not yet had time to spread out and do its awful damage. There had been a lot of water in the creek. As later testimony will show, the rise was both gradual and sudden. Apparently there were two major waves—the first about five feet high and the second about thirty feet high.

The boxing effect of the gorge plus the explosive surge out of the canyon turned the full power of the flood away from Gate Cottage, away from the Bandy residence.

It almost certainly saved the lives of the David Eby family, next in the path downstream.

Their home was sufficiently to the right of the full force so that when it was hit, it moved off its foundation and slammed against the mountain. And there it came to rest, mercifully spared from the total disintegration it surely would have suffered had it been closer to the creek.

The night before, Barbara Eby's parents had visited them. In their conversation they had asked themselves, "What would it be like if the dam ever broke?" Their discussion, the Ebys say, was not because of any real distrust of the creek, but because of the rising water in the creek. They visualized the damage much as it occurred hours later. But not once did they conceive of the dreadful toll of lives that would be taken.

"God is our refuge and strength, a very present help in trouble. Therefore we will not fear . . . though the waters . . . roar and be troubled . . . ."

PSALM 46:1-3

---

1 *Achieving the Impossible With God*, Moothart, 1956, Toccoa Falls College, Toccoa Falls, Georgia. Used by Permission.

SEVEN SECONDS
IN FORREST HALL

Across the creek there was also drama in the corridors of Forrest Hall. Kenny Carroll, a lanky lad from Maryland, dashed out of his room and ran the wrong way—toward certain death.

Kenny had arrived home from a date with Marcia Rees late that evening. Because so much water was coming over the falls he wanted to see it, so he walked up the landscaped path into the canyon and gazed at the thundering falls. The time was about twelve midnight. He observed that the landscaped Rose Garden was underwater. Carroll did not know it, but he was in imminent danger as the dam had already begun to give way.

After returning to Forrest Hall and retiring for the night, he was abruptly awakened. He heard sloshing and thought some of the guys were fooling around in the shower again. But when the water began to rush in around his feet he knew differently. As it rose higher and higher he thought, "I'll be dead if I slip."

In the hall he turned the wrong way and ran into fellow students Bobby Carter and Jon Kerr. They turned him around and the trio headed for a door leading into the stairwell. They reached the door about the same time and all three seemed to squeeze through it at once. Carroll estimates that the series of events involved only seven to ten seconds.

Forrest Hall is a four-story brick dormitory with a capacity (at that time) of 147 students. Normally, when all were present, 127 men were in residence. On the weekend of the flood, however, there were fewer.

Forrest Hall was situated far enough to the east of the water's fury that it was not structurally damaged. But the water rose fast.

Chuck Dowell, a cheerful redhead from Ohio, recalls that in seconds water penetrated the lower floor. Windows collapsed with the pressure as he lunged toward the door.

Had the windows not popped out as they did the whole first floor would have collapsed. The bearing walls for three more floors of dormitory space would then have been gone. Easily, seventy-five men could have died.

Dowell still does not recall how he got into the corridor. Later his door was discovered to be jammed solid and had to be broken down.

Chuck's first recollection was reaching for the yellow trash can in the basement hallway. The water was very mucky and the pockets of the cutoffs he was wearing were later found to be filled with slime. Chuck made it to the stairs, clambered up and got outside; then he headed for the girls' dorm to make sure his girlfriend was safe.

Gerry Brittin, Rick Swires, and Cary Hanna were not so fortunate. Locked in their rooms by the rising water, they were trapped. Only one body was found in the dormitory. One was found about a half-mile away and the other nearly five miles away.

Friends relate that a few days earlier Cary Hanna had talked with them about heaven. Perhaps he was waiting and thinking about the eternal shore. As it turned out, the wait was not long.

Rick was planning to be married and the date was set for June 3, 1978. But maybe he too had sensed something, because he had spoken about the possibility of his dying.

Gerry was a pastor's son from Olean, New York. A dedicated student, he had been hard at work on his senior paper and turned in early, as was his custom.

The juggernaut howled on, leaving in its wake travail and terror in Forrest Hall.

The edge of the flood ripped at the side of the music building. Quickly the side gave way. Thirteen pianos swirled away and doors and furniture were tossed about. The damage was severe, but not complete—because the full force of the flood went elsewhere. And fortunately no one was in the music building.

The unrestrained waters headed for Morrison Hall. Once it had been used for cows, and later when it had become unfit for cows, someone joshed, it had been used for boys! Now it was directly in the flood path. The wood frame structure was no match for the wall of water, bouncing boulders, and surging mud. Trees turned into battering rams. Morrison Hall was swept away. Fortunately, again, it was an empty building, not in use. No lives were lost.

At the edge of the flood, the waters clawed at the hillside. They nearly reached the graves of Dr. and Mrs. R. A. Forrest, who had begun the college in 1907. In 1911 the school was moved to Toccoa Falls.

Two years later, in 1913, Haddock Inn, where Toccoa Falls College was first housed, had burned to the ground. R. A. Forrest was stunned but hardly ready to quit. As he idly poked a stick through the ashes, God spoke to him with these words from Isaiah 61:3: ". . . to provide for those who grieve in Zion, to bestow on them a crown of beauty instead of ashes, the oil of joy instead of mourning, and a garment of praise instead of a spirit of despair; that they might be called oaks of righteousness, a planting of the Lord, that He may be glorified."

He believed the thought was from God and went on to rebuild Toccoa Falls College, confident it was not to end in ashes, confident it was indeed "the planting of the Lord." He also became convinced that a certain psalm was very special: ". . . we went through fire and through water, but you brought us to a place of abundance." (Psalm 66:12)

Forrest believed he had been through his "fire." The developments in the intervening years would have no doubt been beyond his dreams. And he lived until 1957, long enough to see many of his hopes realized.

It appears to have remained for the administration of Dr. Kenn Opperman, who became president in 1974, to go with the college "through water."

Opperman believed, as Forrest and Bandy believed before him, that the school would emerge, as the psalm implies, into a "place of abundance."

As this account unfolds, it will be seen that unusual events have indeed followed the disaster.

Even if the waters had reached the founders' graves, they could not, of course, have touched Dr. and Mrs. Forrest. They themselves, as they so long had taught and known, were "absent from the body . . . present with the Lord." But the hungry waters hurtled on—to devour the living.

Next in order, and directly in line, was Ralls Hall, also unoccupied. A long frame building with large windows, nothing could save it from becoming kindling, from being added to the now deadly burden of flotsam and debris that was aimed malevolently at the residences downstream.

Interestingly enough, Dave and Barbara Eby had lived in Ralls Hall when it was used as a high school dormitory. At that time twenty-eight boys had been housed there plus the five members of the Eby family.

But the high school had been closed. Great difficulties had hindered and obstructed the continuation of high school education on the college campus. The decision to close was not uncontested, however, and feelings ran high. One man, not identified, held Dr. Opperman to blame. Moreover, he held a deep resentment against the college president.

After the flood he wrote to ask forgiveness and to apologize. He was sure that had the academy not been closed his son would have been among the fatalities. Indeed, he might have been. Ralls was in the center of the fury. No one could have survived. The next day not even a trace of the foundation was left.

To the left of the descending torrent sat the guardhouse, a lightweight wooden structure just big enough for two security guards. Jim Conaway and Paul Tate had been on duty there. Aware that the firemen were monitoring the water levels, they had felt no particular concern.

Then they left to go up to the food service area in the basement of LeTourneau Hall to check the compressors on the freezers. While the guards were inspecting the freezers, their security shack was swept away.

Jim Conaway had heard a very loud noise, which he had taken to be the wind. He had complained, "That's all we need after all this rain—a big wind!" But when the guards noticed the bushes weren't moving they knew it wasn't wind and quickly stepped outside.

They were anxious now, so they rushed down to look over the wall between Seby Jones Library and Fant Hall. Ordinarily, the gurgling creek lay below.

But Conaway, especially, was stunned by what he saw through the darkness. "There was enough water," he says, "to scare the living daylights out of me."

Where the flimsy shack that they had just vacated moments before had been, there was now a lake.

My times are in your hand.

PSALM 31:15

CHAPTER 4

THE WATER
TURNS RED

Eldon Elsberry, a 36-year-old Nebraskan, splashed across one of the front yards in Residence Row, a series of houses located near the creek. The water was rising, and just as he reached the road connecting the bridge to Trailerville he heard a noise like a shotgun. It was an electric fuse. The 6100-watt line bringing power into the campus had gone out. Seconds later there was another bang—the second fuse had blown. Elsberry and Fire Chief Dave Fledderjohann could not know it, but the transformer had already toppled at Gate Cottage and horror was heading their way.

Elsberry said, "Dave, what would cause the fuses to blow?"

"I don't know," responded Fledderjohann.

But they both felt apprehension.

Suddenly the black water all around them turned red from the Georgia clay.

Earlier the security guards on campus had been concerned about the rising waters in Toccoa Creek. Their concern had focused on the bridge that gave sole access to the residential sections and to Trailerville. It appeared that the bridge might wash out; and at one point the water had risen about a foot or so above the deck of the bridge. About 12:15 a.m. guard Jim Conaway had called Eldon Elsberry. Eldon, in turn, had contacted David Fledderjohann.

Earlier still, when Elsberry had returned to the campus, he noticed that the steel gate on the alternate entrance was open. He felt some concern. It was always closed after dark so that all traffic had to pass security.

Near the gymnasium, he encountered Fledderjohann, who assured him that there was no fire, but that the water was rising.

Elsberry went home at that point and changed into fireman's gear. The water over the bridge seemed lower, only eight or nine inches deep now, but still they remembered the creek which had flooded in the past. Present by that time were some other members of the department: Ron Ginther, Bill Ehrensberger, and Dee Pinney.

About 10:30 p.m. Ron Ginther casually mentioned Kelly Barnes Dam, and it was decided to go up and check. Taking the fire department vehicle, David and Ron went up and visually inspected the road and the dam. They noticed that the water inside the dam was quite far down and apparently in no danger of overflowing. They radioed back by citizen's band that the dam was solid and that there was no need for concern or alarm.

After they had come back, Elsberry went over to Fledderjohann's vehicle and leaned on the door.

"What did you find?" said Elsberry. Fledderjohann replied, "It's as normal as ever. I've seen it much higher many times."

And the water continued to recede until it was once again flowing under the bridge to Trailerville.

Fledderjohann and Elsberry went home. Just when Elsberry was about to retire, the phone rang. It was Jim Conway at the guard shack.

Conway was concerned because the bridge seemed unstable.

Concluding the telephone conversation, Elsberry said, "I'll talk to David Fledderjohann."

Then Elsberry phoned David. Neither felt any sense of danger, but they decided to check again.

Bill Ehrensberger also came out. His wife and children were all asleep in the house. In Ron Ginther's trailer the light was still on. He and his wife invited the rest of the firemen to come in about 1:00 a.m.

After coffee and cookies the firemen left. They noticed that the water seemed to be rising again. The horizontal yellow stripe on Elsberry's boots had been clearly visible when they had sloshed to Ginther's trailer. Now the yellow stripe could not be seen.

One of the firemen, Dee Pinney, lingered and fussed with a ham radio.

Outside, sensing impending danger, Fledderjohann decided to move two families threatened by the rising creek—the Sproulls and the Woerners. Their houses were lowest in the residential areas and the Sproulls' house was likely to be flooded if the waters continued to rise.

Fledderjohann went to Sproulls' and Dr. Jerry Sproull came to the door. He hesitated and was reluctant to leave, but finally said, "Let me get some clothes."

At this juncture the fuses blew and the explosions reverberated through the valley. Then abruptly the water turned red—and ominous.

Elsberry wheeled to see a wave of water four or five feet high rolling along soundlessly like rapids. "Look out!" he shouted. "There's a wall of water!"

Fledderjohann shouted back to Bill Ehrensberger and Elsberry, "Try to get back across the creek and sound the alarm."

Ehrensberger made it to their truck—on the driver's side. Elsberry ran through the deepening water to the truck only scant feet away. But the furious water hit as he reached the back of the truck. All he could do was grab it. Then he clambered in.

As the water kept coming, Ehrensberger floorboarded the old army vehicle. Surprisingly it still functioned. The two firemen headed for the bridge—still hoping to sound the alarm.

But it was too late. The raging water pushed the truck sideways and threatened to topple it. Since it had a canvas top, both men realized they could not stay in it.

Elsberry said, "We've got to get out of this," and threw himself out of the door. Ehrensberger agreed, but since there was really nowhere safe to go, he was hesitant. When he finally stepped out, his hip boots apparently filled with water at once. The current immediately pulled his feet from under him, and as he swept by Elsberry their outstretched hands missed by eight inches. Bill Ehrensberger was never seen alive again.

Meanwhile, Elsberry had grabbed a tree. But then the tree gave way and the current sucked him under. He says, "I took a big breath and I had one thought—get those boots off."

The fair-haired Nebraskan continues, "I felt power. I know the feeling—I've run heavy equipment; I've ridden bucking horses. But this was POWER. I got one hip boot off. I was on the ground underwater when something—I think it was the Jeep—pinned my right foot. I thought, 'Is this how I am going to die?' Then the object moved. I yanked and came loose.

"I got my second boot off, even though I felt I was in a rolling barrel. I felt held under, and I thought, 'This can't be it, I'm too young to die.' But I felt at peace.

"The clear thought came, 'You do what you can. If you get out, okay. If not, okay.'

"Then there was super peace—sensed, if not thought.

"At that point I ran into something on the bottom. It split my lip and loosened my teeth, and as I came up, I was caught again. I was standing up, but still underwater and glued to a rock.

"Then I came loose again, so I started swimming. I was short of air but I knew I was close to the surface. When I broke through, I got mud—and a little air.

"I swam again until I popped to the surface, gasping and spitting. I knew that the creek had a bend and I felt that I could get out there, so I headed for the bank. I snagged a vine but it started to give. To my right was debris, so I scrambled up about three feet over the rubble, and found myself on level ground, just about sixteen feet above the normal creek level.

"I crawled three or four feet. I was tired and choking. But when the water started to rise again, I got up and ran up the road about twenty steps more.

"Then there was a terrific noise. The big gas main into the college had burst and the released pressure sent a geyser spouting thirty-five feet into the air." Somehow, in the drizzly darkness, Elsberry could see.

"I looked back across the creek and watched the Veer home collapse outward. The roof fell in. I had moved through all that water and now, in a few seconds, I was on the far bank.

"Then I remembered that Bill Ehrensberger had said his wife and children were all sleeping. I ran for their frame home hoping to warn them, but halfway there I saw it begin to float away.

"The agony was awful. I knew a man's wife and children were floating away. Then the trailers started to go. They looked like tractor trailers pulling out onto the freeway—they really took off and started to fly. They were okay unless they hit each other.

"There were many screams, mostly from children. I stood on the bank and watched people die, but I couldn't do a thing."

Trailerville had become a lake.

In retrospect, Elsberry says he had two big problems. Living with what his ears heard and understanding why. But time has changed his perspective.

Though Elsberry had been a minister before taking up his maintenance role at the College, he now says that the experiences during the flood have not damaged his Christian faith but made it stronger.

One more thing, Elsberry did not live in Trailerville. His family was safe on higher ground. He didn't have to be in the path of this hellish water—but he was.

You will keep in perfect peace all who trust in you,
all whose thoughts are fixed on you!

ISAIAH 26:3, NLT

I DIDN'T WANT DADDY TO DIE

When Thad Fledderjohann, 3, got up the morning of November 6, he wanted to know why his mommie had been crying.

She said, "I was crying because Daddy was killed last night. But he's okay, he's with Jesus. I'm only crying because I miss him."

When her son Brian, 4, heard about the disaster he got angry. "I didn't want the dam to break," he said. "I didn't want Daddy to die."

Then they all cried together.

Thad and Brian's daddy, David Fledderjohann, was singled out as the hero who died in the Toccoa Falls tragedy. And he was that.

His last words to his men were, "Try to get back across the creek and sound the alarm."

Fledderjohann seemed to be drawn to emergencies. He inclined toward helping others; and the six-foot young man from Ohio might indeed be embarrassed were he to know that the media paid so much attention to his heroism.

In the November 16 Memorial Service, Dr. Kenn Opperman, college president, said it succinctly: "David Fledderjohann did not have to go into the flood area. He was there helping people because he felt he ought to go." And Opperman continued, "We believe the young people from Toccoa Falls College will always be that way. They will be willing to go with the gospel of Jesus Christ—even if they don't come back."

Margaret Fledderjohann, David's widow, had been an MK—a missionary's kid—in Nicaragua, the Honduras, and Mexico. Her Spanish accent is still authentic when she cares to use it. She met David at Toccoa Falls College, and they were married at the end of David's junior year. Before graduation Dave joined the staff of the college print shop where he became the manager. He also enjoyed paramedical and civil defense courses.

Dave was the first of his family to come south to Toccoa, but others have come since. The Greater Europe Mission once called him to go to Europe as a missionary. On another occasion Taylor University asked him to develop their print shop operation in Indiana, but he didn't go. Somehow he didn't feel his work was done. Nor was it—till the early morning hours of November 6, 1977.

Margaret says God has given her joy and peace after her loss. With dry eyes and deep earnestness she says it and it rings true.

The key to her present serenity probably goes back to an earlier time in her relationship with David. She remembers fearing that she would get a phone call informing her that David was dead. Believing it her Christian duty to give her husband completely to God, she did exactly that. There was deep peace then. And in her present bereavement, the peace remains.

It was raining hard the night of the tragedy. David had looked in the door about 9:00 p.m. He said he was watching the Sproull home and the bridge. Margaret put the children to bed and sat down to write two letters—one to her parents, another to David's parents. She told them that it had been raining for a few days and that David was out on duty. When David came in at 11:30 they spent a last hour together, but at 12:30 he was called out again. The guard thought perhaps the bridge to Trailerville was going to wash out.

About 3:00 a.m. Margaret heard the telephone ring. The call was from a friend in Toccoa. "Are you all right?" she asked Margaret. Mrs. Fledderjohann was puzzled at the question, but said yes.

While she was still on the phone, she saw the fire truck wheel into the driveway and heard a knock on the door. It was Dee Pinney, who came in with a shaken, hurt look on his face. He told Margaret that the dam had broken and that David was missing.

Margaret asked, "Was David on foot?" When she learned he was, she had little hope that he was still alive.

Dee had brought a couple of girls with him who were waiting outside in the fire truck. He asked Margaret if she would like them to stay with her.

She agreed and Dee went to get them. Dee then left, and the two girls remained with Margaret the rest of the night. The girls told her they had heard the explosions from the fuses and also the rush of the water. While they waited, there was prayer, some tears, and the reading of the Bible.

At about 4:00 a.m. Doyle Fledderjohann, Dave's brother, came down to use the phone, since the Fledderjohann home was in one of the areas of the campus where the phones still functioned. He walked in so naturally that it was clear he didn't know that David was missing. But an hour and a half later he identified David's body at the hospital.

When informed, Margaret's first reaction was, "This is not real. David always comes back from helping people." Then Scriptures came flooding to her mind. "Heaven and earth shall pass away, but my words shall not pass away." "Absent from the body . . . present with the Lord."

Margaret Fledderjohann, still reeling from shock and sorrow, got down on her knees and impulsively said, "Thank you, Lord, that the dam broke." She was acting on a biblical principle—"In everything give thanks."

And she prayed again, "Lord, teach me how to mourn. I can't

sit down and analyze my feelings. Show me when to cry and what to cry about.

"I knew David was in the presence of the Lord," she said. "Nothing has made it clearer to me that all we have been taught and have believed all these years is a reality.

"Joy and peace were the two most outstanding things that came to me. When I asked the Lord for strength, I got joy. I thought it was fantastic. The joy of the Lord really is our strength.

"Saint Paul wrote to the Christians who were being burned and severed in pieces and persecuted in many other ways. And he said, 'Rejoice in the Lord always.' I've noticed the Bible is full of peace and joy passages—all addressed to suffering believers.

"The knowledge that God loves us and that anything that comes into our lives is through love is very precious. He does it in love."

The funeral in Toccoa's First Alliance Church was a celebration of victory. Ten victims of the flood, including David, were remembered.

Upon arrival at the cemetery, Margaret Fledderjohann asked church organist Nona Carlson if she thought it would be all right for them to sing at the service.

Mrs. Carlson decided to check with the officiating minister, Rev. Merle Graven. "Certainly," he said.

And so at the cemetery, upon completion of the prayer by Dr. Paul Alford, Mrs. Carlson began to sing softly.

It will be worth it all, when we see Jesus.
Life's trials will seem so small, when we see Christ.
One glimpse of His dear face, all sorrow will erase;
So bravely run the race, 'til we see Christ.

"WHEN WE SEE CHRIST" | AUTHOR: ESTHER KERR RUSTHOI
© 1940 NEW SPRING (ADMIN. BY BRENTWOOD-BENSON MUSIC PUBLISHING, INC.)

Some of the bereaved began to join in the singing.

A reporter/photographer from Athens, Georgia, couldn't understand why there was such joy. When asked if he would like someone to help him find what these incredible people had, he said yes. So in a praying, weeping huddle, a newsman at the funeral called upon the Lord.

Still later a salesman who used to make calls to the print shop came by to see Margaret. He just wanted to tell her that, through David's life and passing, he too had found the Lord.

* * *

Dee Pinney was a lanky Pennsylvanian, 26 years old, who worked with David Fledderjohann in the college print shop. He was also a member of the Volunteer Fire Department. In that capacity he participated in the creek-watch.

He also went in for coffee at the Ginthers'. Because he was interested in electronics, he stayed a bit longer than the other firemen to tinker with the ham radio.

About 1:20 a.m. he left the Ginther home to cross to the other side of the creek. But as he drove across the bridge the campus power went out, so he set out to look for an electrician and a fire truck.

Unknowingly, he drove along the creek road—straight toward the descending flood. At that time the dam had probably already given way, and the destruction was about to begin. For Pinney it appeared first as about six inches of water lapping down the road and against Forrest Hall. It was moving rapidly.

Instantly he thought, "The dam broke!"

He rammed his car into reverse. By then the water was to the floorboards. Soon the backup lights were covered and he struck a tree. The water was knee-deep when he clambered out of his car, and almost immediately it was to his waist.

Carefully, very carefully, because he couldn't swim, Dee

Pinney moved up the hill toward Stewart Hall, another large, frame building on campus.

About the time he reached Stewart Hall, he heard electrical wires falling into the water and then an explosion. He forced himself to work his way toward the center of campus. The wall of water was storming by in all its raging power.

He headed for the fire department, and as he crossed the campus a student asked if he should ring the iron bell. Pinney consented since there was no electricity to sound any other alarm. Then, in a state of near-shock, he moved to the fire hall, took out the truck, and sounded the siren as he headed for the hospital.

He tried to call his sister Eloise in Trailerville and thought he heard someone pick up the phone, but then it went dead. A nurse at the hospital called the ambulance and Pinney called 911 and told the operator to summon the Fire Department in Toccoa and also the Civil Defense.

Apparently, Eloise, Dee's twin sister, had called the telephone operator at about 1:30 a.m. She thought she had heard an explosion and imagined that the print shop was on fire.

When it became clear that a flood was involved, Eloise apparently left the trailer and headed her car for Upper Trailerville and safety. But the car must have stalled. In any case, Eloise did not escape.

She was a quiet girl whose off-campus job was at Sherino's, a local Italian restaurant. Many customers and fellow workers came to her funeral.

Pinney's first thought at the hospital was that he was the only fireman who survived. But when Eldon Elsberry came in crying, he knew he wasn't alone.

Pinney went to the Opperman home and placed a call to Dr. Opperman, who was in Florida at that time. When Opperman came on the line Pinney told him what he could. "I'm sure some people are gone," he said.

Pinney proceeded to the Fledderjohann home to tell Margaret that Dave was missing. He couldn't bring himself to tell her that Dave was dead, although he felt sure that was the case.

He did not want to go back to the flood area. A lot of other help was on the scene then and there seemed to be no need. He had been calling a friend in Toccoa, Mrs. Nona Carlson, who had herself been bereaved a couple of years earlier and was close to Dee and Eloise. Pinney ended up at Mrs. Carlson's home, and it was from her that he heard the news that Eloise, his twin, was gone.

It was like losing a part of himself.

And so, dear brothers and sisters, I plead with you to give your bodies to God because of all he has done for you. Let them be a living and holy sacrifice—the kind he will find acceptable. This is truly the way to worship him. Don't copy the behavior and customs of this world, but let God transform you into a new person by changing the way you think. Then you will learn to know God's will for you, which is good and pleasing and perfect.

ROMANS 12:1-2, NLT

II. RESIDENCE ROW

CHAPTER 6

KITTIES IN HEAVEN?

There were some little folks (five of them to be exact) at the Pepsnys', the first house on Residence Row. Three little visitors and two who lived there. Kitties and bicycles were very important to them, but the Savior was too. What they didn't know was that the gates of heaven were already ajar.

Once past Morrison and Ralls, the wall of water, burdened with bobbing autos, loaded with debris, and probably moving at one hundred miles an hour, hurled itself through the narrow valley like a freight train out of control.

In the green and scenic valley, not much more than a hundred feet wide, sat Residence Row. Nestled beside the cheerful brook, it was the choice place to live on the campus at Toccoa Falls College.

The houses there were frame and brick. One was gray. Another coral. Another rose. There were fences and cars. Clipped lawns and tended flowers. Boats and trailers. A mobile home with a frame addition was located there too. There were carports and shrubbery. Behind one house was an empty rabbit pen. A tool shed stood behind another. The street was improved.

It was this area of the campus that was to bear the full fury of the water. The first wall of water came through carrying boats and fences and trees before it. The water raced on to the bridge over Georgia's Route 17 where it was momentarily stopped, and though some of the water continued on toward Lake Hartwell, a backwash started back up toward Trailerville and Residence Row.

Observers on the scene believe that when the main wall of water, at least thirty feet high, lunged through the narrow valley it slammed into the smaller wave on its way back. The furious collision of those two waves hurled debris about one hundred feet above the normal level of the creek.

It was toward this sleeping campus suburb the howling water rushed that dark morning of November 6.

Edward and Carol Pepsny were new at Toccoa Falls College, and their home was the first in Residence Row to face the onslaught. Ed was a graduate of Asbury Seminary in Wilmore, Kentucky, and originated from Nashville, Tennessee. He had taken his undergraduate training at Case Western Reserve University in Cleveland, Ohio.

While he studied astronomy there with a college friend, the topic sometimes turned to religion. Christianity, Ed's friend decided, ought to be worth everything or nothing at all.

He soon decided it was worth everything and promptly sought to persuade Ed. One day he handed Ed a gospel tract.

Pepsny stuffed the tract into his pocket and proceeded to a Roman Catholic church to attend mass. Arriving a while before the service began, he drew out the tract, read it, and immediately made the same full commitment to Christ that his friend had made.

It was a major step on the path that led him to Toccoa Falls College.

He had begun to teach at Toccoa Falls College in January 1977 and had only moved onto the campus in the summer. Ed and Carol had two children—Paul, 5, and Bonnie, 2. Theirs was a quiet home, and it was easily apparent that they were a loving, close-knit family.

Ed and Carol Pepsny were very private people, but yet hospitable. They had invited Debbie Jones, 19, to stay in their home; and had she not been at work she too would have been lost in the flood.

Debbie and Carol had often talked about death and dying. About heaven, too.

Carol had once had a nightmare about her small boy drowning, and sometimes she seemed apprehensive about the creek. Debbie taught Carol and both the children to swim the previous summer. But it didn't, it couldn't, help the morning of November 6.

Edward Pepsny still had not completed a full year of teaching Greek on the campus when the disaster struck. The night before the flood Carol Pepsny had felt the burden to pray instead of sleep. The Pepsnys did not know the reason for the desire to pray, they simply wanted to do so. They had also decided to fast on Saturday as a more earnest form of spiritual desire. Apparently, they were fasting when the waters descended upon them.

Ed and Carol were friendly with the Jerry Sproull family, and when the waters began to threaten the Sproull home, Dr. Sproull took his three girls to the Pepsney residence. It was on higher ground and, he thought, not likely to be flooded at all.

The Sproull girls, Melissa, Jocelyn, and Joanna, cried a bit. Somehow they didn't want to spend the night away from their parents. But Jerry Sproull had been firm. He wanted to protect his precious children.

What he could not know was that he placed them squarely in the path of the raging waters. At 1:27 a.m., when the roaring flood descended, Ed Pepsny's little family and another man's dear children were all carried away. No one could survive the center of the rushing flood. And no one did.

Seven fatalities in one awful stroke. But surely angels attended the homegoing of a man of God, his wife, and five tiny believers.

Though hardly a brick was left, the little one who wanted to know if there were bicycles in heaven found out, and the tiny girl who wanted to know if there were kitties in heaven found out, too.

Let the little children come to me, and do not hinder them, for the kingdom of God belongs to such as these.

LUKE 18:16

CHAPTER 7

SOMETHING WONDERFUL

The rage of the waters was not assuaged. The next residence in the doomed row lay right in the path of the fury and was also angrily swallowed. It belonged to Paul and Mary Williams.

How "Uncle Paul" and "Aunt Mary" met death we cannot know, but we can surmise that they met it as they did life, with serenity and equanimity.

Uncle Paul was a Texan. He met Aunt Mary at Toccoa Falls College, and though she briefly served as a missionary in Cuba, she came back promptly to marry Uncle Paul. Just as promptly, he took her back to Texas and stayed there twenty years.

But the pull of Toccoa Falls College and the hearty charisma of R. A. Forrest proved irresistible. They came back. Uncle Paul was wise. Philosophical. Will Rogers-like. And dear to students, staff, and faculty alike.

Aunt Mary was the kind who brought cookies to the guard shack for cold and lonely boys. The day before the flood she had given a married student, Jim Weiss, a ball of popcorn.

When there was a vacancy on the Board of Trustees at Toccoa

Falls College, Uncle Paul was nominated.

Aunt Mary was the director of Christian Service for women for more than twenty years. At the time she died she had in her purse $100 in Christian Service funds for the purchase of materials. When her purse was found after the flood the money was intact.

Aunt Mary not only directed Christian Service activities, she participated in them. At the hospital, in the schools, and in town, doors were opened because she cared for people.

Dr. Opperman affirmed that sometimes at the end of the month when there was no way to meet the payroll for the college, Uncle Paul would walk in and lay a check on his desk. His resources were on the line for God.

When Uncle Paul was alive he always had appropriate stories, but he has a completely new story now. The grown children of Uncle Paul and Aunt Mary call them blessed. Their lengthy lives are over and their bodies rest on the hillside near the graves of Dr. and Mrs. R. A. Forrest.

The college that affectionately called them Uncle and Aunt honored them in death.

Just the Friday before the flood, Aunt Mary saw the Rev. Nathan Penland, executive director of Alumni Affairs, in the campus post office. He may have looked downcast, because Aunt Mary said, "Don't get discouraged, Nate. I know we all do at times. Paul and I really believe God is going to meet the school real soon in a very unusual way. We don't know exactly what He's going to do, but it's going to be wonderful."

And wonderful it was! For godly people with heaven in view.

... no good thing does he withhold from
those whose walk is blameless.

PSALM 84:11

CHAPTER 8

I'M READY TO DIE TOMORROW

A dozen dead? Yes, certainly, but the flood sought twenty-seven more. Dr. Jerry Sproull's home was next in the row, with no hope at all of withstanding the onslaught of gathering debris, the awful power of a wall of water thirty feet high.

When the water turned red, David Fledderjohann had gone to Sproulls' to warn them. Ever the fireman at heart, as Ehrensberger had tried to get away in the jeep, and as the water surged upward, Fledderjohannn urged the Sproulls to clamber onto the furniture in the house to keep away from the raging flood. But there was no escape, and at the last Jerry prayed desperately, "O God—it's all in Your hands now." Little did he know that Melissa, Jocelyn, and Joanna, his little girls, were already in God's hands.

Pat Sproull had married Jerry in 1965. Their marriage lasted just a little over twelve years, but it was the kind of union that allowed Jerry to lecture regularly about family relationships. He had no fear that his audiences would be disappointed by his own marriage.

As the waters rose irresistibly in the Sproull home, Pat placed her hand on the window and found it inexplicably open. The air conditioner had been sucked outward.

Then the water pulled at Mrs. Sproull too. She was a slender woman but she remembers turning her head to let herself slip through the open window.

When she surfaced she put her hand down. Shingles! She thought, "This is the proverbial riding the roof!" But as she rode it she reasoned, "God must have something left for me. I've made it this far."

Then the roof collided with a demolished trailer. Again she was hurled into the water—but this time she grabbed a board, then a limb. Bill Anderson, another of the victims, finally pulled her out and she soon found herself huddled in the woods with a small group of survivors. They were slimy and some cases naked, but there was singing, prayer, Scripture, and, incredibly, some joshing and humor. Mrs. Sproull, though battered and injured, helped care for the children.

Pat Sproull clung to the Twenty-Third Psalm: "Even though I walk through the valley of the shadow of death, I will fear no evil, for you are with me; your rod and your staff, they comfort me. You prepare a table before me in the presence of my enemies. You anoint my head with oil; my cup overflows. Surely goodness and love will follow me all the days of my life, and I will dwell in the house of the Lord forever."

Later in the hospital when the news came to Pat that all her children were gone, one nurse said, "Pat, how can you be so strong? You've lost all your babies tonight." Through her tears and brokenness she sustained her colleagues. (She was a supervisory nurse at Stephens County Hospital.) And she gave her friends an answer—"We gave our girls to God long ago, even before they were born. He's just taken them now."

Pat related that Jerry used to talk about heaven. He looked forward to it. His inquisitive legal mind craved some of the details the Bible leaves unrecorded. Perhaps, she thought, Jerry didn't think he would grow old. She felt that had he known what was going to happen at Toccoa Falls College, had he thought his death could have brought revival to the school or led someone to faith in Christ, he would have been willing to die. Jerry jogged and prayed every morning, and as he jogged he prayed for Toccoa Falls College.

Pat Sproull struggled in her sorrow. She said, "I've lost everything. I don't know whether I'll ever be happy again. But there's joy. God gives me joy. There is a difference.

"Some books show only the bright side. And readers think, 'Those people can't be real!' But I loved my family. I'm crying and I'm still crying."

When America's First Lady Rosalynn Carter came to the campus Sunday afternoon, she visited Mrs. Sproull in the Stephens County Hospital. There, in Mrs. Sproull's room, the two women quoted the Twenty-Third Psalm together.

Some wept at Toccoa Falls College and some rejoiced. Perhaps that is as it should be. Pat Sproull still weeps.

But through her tears, or perhaps because of them, she has been able to reach out to others in a new way.

In her duties at Stephens County Hospital, Pat Sproull dealt with life and death every day. Before the flood she had always felt unable to bring comfort to those who had lost loved ones. She used to busy herself with details to avoid dealing with bereaved people. Now, she seeks to minister comfort to families.

Shortly after the flood she encountered a woman who had lost her husband. The woman was weeping and taking her loss very hard.

"I know how you feel," said Mrs. Sproull softly.

The woman looked at her as if to say, "How could you?"

Then Pat told her about November 6. The two women embraced and wept together.

"For the first time I felt I could help the bereaved," says Mrs. Sproull. "For the first time I could feel for them."

Dr. Sproull may have sensed that the end was near. The day before the tragedy he was into one of his frequent theological discussions with a student. In the course of the conversation with the student he said, "I'm ready to die tomorrow."

And he did.

But before he died he had written an article and suggested that it be published anonymously. It was called, "So That the Poor Mourn."

It was published in the Memorial Edition of *TFC Today*—but not anonymously, as Jerry hoped. The thrust of the article is that beside a man's open grave there should be a company of grieving poor who were helped in his lifetime. Jerry urged worthwhile living so that it might finally be said, "The poor were sorry when he died." The article's final sentence was, "Dear God, may the poor be sorry when I die."

Dr. Gerald McGraw, friend and colleague on the Toccoa faculty, could not help but respond, "We are sorry, Jerry. We are richer because you lived, and our loss is immense."

Blessed are those who mourn, for they will be comforted.

MATTHEW 5:4

CHAPTER 9

LA SUERTE DE ALGUNOS

Betty Jean Woerner was secretary to Dr. Kenn Opperman, and when I was a guest at Toccoa Falls College seven weeks before the flood, she was helpful to me as well. Since she had been a missionary to Chile along with her husband Ray, she knew Spanish and we tossed around some phrases. I distinctly remember her saying, "La suerte de algunos." It means, "The luck of some people."

What happened the dark morning of November 6 had nothing to do with fate or chance, Betty Jean would certainly affirm.

The Woerners had been missionaries with The Christian and Missionary Alliance in Chile for more than twenty years. On an extended furlough in Georgia, Ray was working in a nearby plant on the night shift. Their four children were home with their mother in Residence Row.

At about 1:15 a.m. Betty Jean still had not gone to bed. She had a phobia about the water. Apparently, while there was no premonition, she respected that creek and seemed to be restless.

She went to her son David's room and told him to move the car away from the rising waters. He groused, half awake, but he pulled on his jeans and went outside. He also shoved a flashlight in his hip pocket.

At that time the water was one foot below the Woerner house. After moving the car, David Woerner headed back to his home, intending to enter through the rear door.

Just then there was a sound like thunder, as the big fuses went out. Denise Woerner was wakened at 1:26 a.m. according to her digital clock. She grabbed her clothes and was outside in about a minute. She saw the rising water and sensed immediately that the dam had burst

As she ran for safety she screamed, "The dam's broken! The dam's broken!" David, in panic, started to run with her—until he realized that his sister Debbie and his mother were not with them. He dashed back to the house to get them. Betty Jean was speechless. Debbie grabbed one arm and David grabbed the other. They ran down the road, futilely as it turned out, because they stayed in the center of the flood path. David still didn't believe the dam had broken.

Denise had sensed it, though. As she ran through Trailerville she kept screaming and, according to one report, thumping trailers hard with her open palm. A number of people who were thus awakened were saved.

Somehow, David, Debbie, and their mother made it to the print shop, a large, solid building, but squarely in the path of the flood. Never once did David think of the safety of the mountain off to his right. Daniel, David's brother, had joined them by this time, but the force of the still-rising waters soon pinned all four of them against the shop wall.

Daniel, a soccer player, sprang free and began to jump from one car roof to another. Like floating checkers, they led him to safety. He shouted for others to follow and his mother broke her silence and cried out, "Daniel, be careful, come back." But Daniel didn't come back. And he escaped.

When the print shop began to crumble behind Betty Jean, David, and Debbie, they pushed a car out into the current and moved out with it. Betty Jean clutched the rear view mirror. David held Debbie.

"Lord, I don't want to die," Debbie cried.

"Don't worry, Debbie," her mother comforted her, "It'll be all right."

Then the big wave hit, carrying everything before it. Debbie screamed and they were gone.

David was plunged under the water twice, then he grabbed a timber which carried him, at about forty miles an hour, straight toward the bank and an ugly pile of debris. But suddenly the current changed. He was not slammed into the cutting edge of he debris. Instead, he scampered over it to safety.

When Ray Woerner returned from work in a local factory shortly after 3:00 a.m., he found he could not cross the bridge on Route 17. There was water and debris everywhere. And a chilling sight that telegraphed disaster—his own trunk, which he had used on the mission field, went floating by. When Dave met him, he told his dad, "I don't know where Mom and Debbie are." But in his heart he knew they had died.

Grief for the Woerners was hard, although it was not always visible. David stated at the time, "I've shed tears twice—but a thousand times a day I've felt the emptiness."

From this deep hurt, however, came an understanding. David believed Christians must weep with those who weep, rejoice with those who rejoice, and have the wisdom and discernment to know the difference.

He summed up his feelings this way, "There's a settled understanding, but grief beyond measure." And Betty Jean and Debbie? For them it was terror at Toccoa Falls College one moment, present with the Lord the next. That's what Saint Paul makes clear.

There are no shocks or bad luck for believers. But surprises, yes. Betty Jean and daughter Debbie, good and godly women, were surprised—by joy.

. . . absent from the body . . . present with the Lord.

2 Corinthians 5:8

CHAPTER 10

THE BABY NEVER MOVED

Jaimée Veer was a breast-fed baby and, according to Sue her mother, she was a very loving child. She cuddled a lot, always searching for her mother's breast. And she was terrified of water.

But the night of the flood Jaimée did not move. She never searched. She never cried. Incredibly, in all of the turmoil, even in the water, she was quiet.

"I believe," Sue affirms, "that God may have taken my baby before the flood came.

"My greatest memory is that of the soft, warm body against me."

Earlier the phone had rung at the Veer home. Sue's husband Doug was a supervisor of maintenance at the college and the call would have taken him away from his family, away from the row of residences lying silently in the flood path. But for some strange reason, no one heard the call and it went unanswered.

About 1:30 a.m. there was a different sound, which they did hear. It was somewhat tinny and hollow. Others have described it as two oceans rushing to reach the same place. Doug jumped up and looked out the window. What he saw looked like a train—but there wasn't supposed to be a train in the valley. Apparently, it was the big wave coming through.

Baby Jaimée was sleeping with her parents. Doug pushed both Sue and the baby up the ladder leading to the attic. By then he was up to his chest in water. Anita, their 14-year-old, was screaming, but the baby did not waken. As the water kept rising, Doug cried out, "My God, I can't get to them all!" He still had not reached his two sons.

Sue heard Doug go under water. She says, "I felt alone. I didn't want to be alone or to die alone." Their frame house with a brick front began to shake, so halfway into the attic she doubled over the baby and covered her.

Suddenly a tree rammed through the trembling house, knocking her off the step. But still Sue Veer clung to her little girl. Under water, Sue could hear the noise of the flood. Still, the baby did not move.

When Mrs. Veer was hit by either a piece of concrete or a tree, she and the baby were flung apart.

Sue tried to fight clear, but she lay under debris. Finally, she took a deep breath. It should have been water, but, unexpectedly, it wasn't. She just blacked out. Then she came up, churning but not coughing, and without water or mud in her lungs.

Suddenly, her face was caught and began to be crushed. She could hear the facial bones cracking. "It was sickening," she says. "I wanted to vomit."

She still couldn't believe what was happening to her. She found herself thinking about the Lord and His suffering on the cross. Then suddenly she was dragged down again.

Next Sue remembers being on her back underwater. She saw lights above her and assumed she was dead. As she floated upward she expected to meet Jesus at any moment.

But when she broke surface she encountered debris and a layer of oily sludge several inches thick clinging to the waters.

She also smelled the reeking odor of escaping gas mixed with mud. She knew she wasn't in heaven yet.

The water was still moving fast. It seemed like fifty or sixty miles per hour. For some reason she thought she was going over the falls.

Whenever an object went by her she shouted, "Get to the shore!" One object answered her. It was her daughter Anita, who immediately dove off the flotsam and came to her mother. They were both naked but alive.

"Momma, we've got to pray," Anita said.

They clambered out of the water and debris in the area of the old farm at the far edge of the flood plain below Trailerville.

"Momma, tell me I'm asleep," said Anita.

But Sue couldn't.

Sue's jaw and facial bones were broken and her cameo-like face was badly swollen. Later, when she was being carried on a stretcher to the hospital, Doug shone a flashlight into her face. He didn't even recognize his own wife, and he said to himself, "That woman can't live."

The medical examiner suspected a broken left leg, spinal injuries, a crushed skull, a broken neck, three broken ribs, and ten broken facial bones.

But as it turned out, after prayer, Sue had only the facial injuries. The other injuries were gone.

When Doug went underwater, he and Sue had become separated. The tree had come pounding through, knocking out the end of the house with a frightening force. Doug, Jr., 18, had cried out, "My God, Dad, help me!" Kirk, 10, had somehow gotten tangled up in a big flag that had fallen off the wall. Later he shot free.

Doug, Sr. later said, "All of us were under water. We all ran out of breath. We all took a huge gasp. We all should have taken in water and mud but God gave us air, and though we all blacked out, we came out without choking."

Doug hit something solid under water. It turned out to be a forklift. Somehow the top part of it was still above water.

Previously Doug had been asked what he would say if God took all his family from him in an accident. He had surmised that he really might blame God to His face in such a situation.

But Doug had misjudged himself. When he broke water at the top of the forklift he cried out, "Dear God, I love you."

For twenty-five minutes he clung there. As forty-five-gallon drums floated by, Doug was tempted to grab one of them. He's glad now he didn't, because he suddenly heard crying and talking.

It was Kirk, his 10-year-old son. "Oh, Daddy," he said, "I'm so cold."

Kirk had felt the door handle of a truck come into his hand underwater. Instinctively he opened it and climbed into the bubble of air. There he survived close to the forklift his father had seized.

He had been praying, "Thank You, God, for the water. Thank You for the flood." And he had wanted to know if it was okay to pray that way. His father assured him, "That's what the Bible says—'In everything give thanks.'"

Kirk went on, "When I was finished praying, I intended to jump back into the water and go to be with Jesus and the rest of you." To him it had just seemed to be the obvious thing for a believing little boy to do.

Kirk and Doug stayed together and the waters began to recede. Fifteen minutes later they walked out. Doug, Jr., climbing onto a broken trailer, had escaped too.

Later Sue had another prayer answered. She wanted very much to attend Jaimée's funeral at Toccoa's First Alliance Church. Though she was confined to the hospital, she saw even the committal service on television. The television clips seemed to be specially edited for her.

"We feel honored to have gone through it," Sue said. "We feel God chose carefully those who were to suffer and still give glory unto Himself. Jaimée was ours. But she is gone. God gave us Jaimée long enough to teach us how to love one another.

Many waters cannot quench love,
rivers cannot sweep it away ....

SONG OF SOLOMON 8:7

CHAPTER 11

ANGUISH
RIPPED AT HIM

The night before the flood, the Ron Ginther family had enjoyed a special time in which the parents had read from *The Silver Chair*, a story by C. S. Lewis from *The Chronicles of Narnia*. The Narnia stories included a tale in which the king died and was raised again.

Ron and Mary Jo had questioned their four little girls carefully. And the children had understood the story's message. What they did not know was that before the night ended all but Ron would perish in the flood—to wait with certainty the coming resurrection.

Shortly after the firemen's coffee break at the Ginthers' home the water began to rise dramatically and alarm seized Ron Ginther. He ran to his mobile home.

"We've got to get out of here!" he told his wife. "I think the dam broke."

But by the time Ron and Mary Jo had aroused their children, the water was already to their knees. In a desperate attempt to escape, Ron kicked out a window, but his flashlight beam fell on gushing water. And inside the mobile home the water continued to rise.

When the trailer began to float, Ron knew they had to get out and a roof section floating by seemed to be the answer.

He placed one of his little girls out on the roof—but she was immediately washed off. Awful anguish ripped at Ron Ginther, but there was no time to mourn their terrible loss.

His wife urged him to go out on the roof himself so he could help the rest of them.

The children had been shouting and screaming, but Mary Jo had assured them, "Jesus is with us, He'll take care of us." Her serenity was remarkable; she was ordinarily afraid of water.

With his second girl Rhonda under his arm, Ron struggled through the window, only to be pinned between his house and the roof. He thought he was going to die right then and remembers praying, "Oh Lord, if this is what You want, I'm ready to meet You."

Suddenly the buildings which were squeezing the life out of him eased apart.

He still had Rhonda under his arm, so they both clambered onto the roof. Then he turned toward his trailer.

But it was gone! Where once had been love, warmth, a beautiful family—nothing!

Residence Row was gone. Obliterated.

Back of that row, pressed in against the mountain, Ron Ginther had tucked his trailer. The mobile home, with a frame addition, lay right in the path of the thundering flood—an onslaught loaded with boulders, trees, even bouncing pianos swept out of the music building upstream. Now it was no more.

So far Ron's struggle to save his family had been a losing one, but he still had Rhonda. Then the roof on which they were precariously perched began to tip, and violent waves began to pound it harder and harder. Finally, a mighty wave crashed into it and his little girl was torn from him.

Ron himself, though hammered by the water, managed to hang on.

He clung there till the fury passed. Later he was able to walk out of the knee-deep water. When Ron joined a group of students and told them his whole family had been drowned, they broke into spontaneous prayer.

Finally he headed for the hospital. He knew within that he had lost his whole family, that Mary Jo and his four small daughters, Brenda, Rhonda, Nancy, and Tracy were gone. Yet he still had peace. "The feeling," he says, "was the most real in my life."

This soft-spoken man, who lost so much, buried his little family not too far from Toccoa Falls College. This was home, and they were happy here. And he said, "If we had to do it all over again, even if we knew the flood was going to come, we'd agree to come here again. This is where God wanted us—I know Mary Jo would feel this way."

Ron Ginther was not trying to be sensational. "We've only been Christians since 1975," he says. "This is how it really is."

For this God is our God for ever and ever;
he will be our guide even to the end.

PSALM 48:14

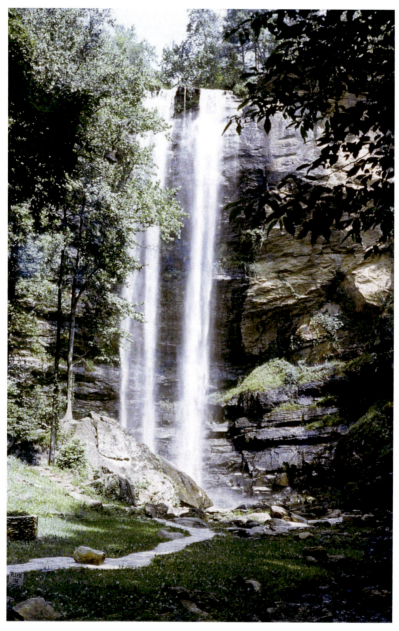

Toccoa Falls prior to the flood

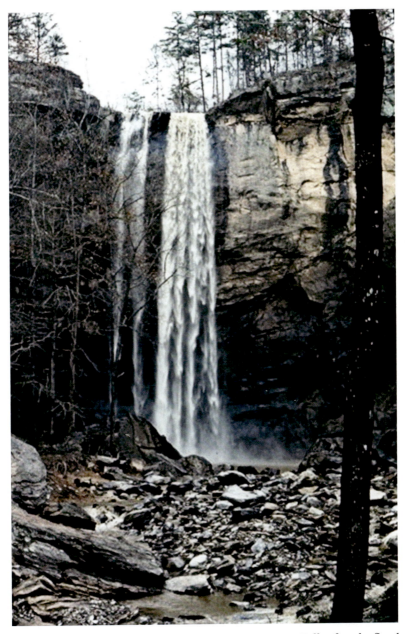

Toccoa Falls after the flood

The empty basin of the Kelly Barnes Lake

The remains of the earthen dam

View of the dam break from lakebed

Aerial view of the path of the flood to Toccoa Falls

Aerial view after the flood of Toccoa Falls, Gate Cottage, and the residence of former college President Dr. Julian Bandy

Gate Cottage still standing after the flood

The path of the flood between the men's dormitory, Forrest Hall, to the left, and the Eby home to the right

Home of the Dave Eby family, where all survived

Site of Ralls Hall, formerly used as a high school dormitory, but vacant on November 6

*Site of the Guard House and Gate, and Residence Row, looking
downstream*

The mute remains of Residence Row, looking upstream

Aerial view of Residence Row, Print Shop and Maintenance Building

*Across the bridge to Residence Row, Print Shop,
Maintenance Building, and Trailerville*

Watermarks on a tree
by the bridge

Print Shop and Maintenance Building

Aerial view of the path of destruction through Trailerville

Twenty-seven trailers were swept away

Path of the Creek through the floodplain

Trailers along the road to Upper Trailerville

The college bus on the floodplain

*Aerial view of the GA Route 17 bridge, which held,
keeping the toll from rising downstream*

The bridge at GA Route 17 forming a secondary dam

*Federal Disaster Coordinator Tom Credle coordinated
all clean-up and repairs*

Cleanup operations were swift and efficient

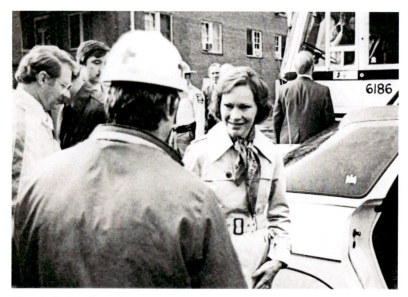

First Lady Rosalynn Carter arriving on campus the afternoon of November 6

*The Press Conference held early afternoon of November 6;
President Opperman (center) is flanked by General Billy Jones
and Governor George Busbee*

*Disaster relief agencies such as the Salvation Army and
the Red Cross were quickly onsite*

III. TRAGEDY IN TRAILERVILLE

THERE IS
STILL PAIN

"The hardest thing to deal with is absence," says Jeff Metzger, 29. "There is still pain. Cassie and Dirksen are not coming back."

There are little reminders that make it hard. It hurts when Jeff sees little children Dirksen's age. On a visit to Pennsylvania, when he saw a couple just brushing snow off a car, he felt it keenly. Cassie and he can't do things together anymore.

Cassie had always told him, "Jeff, you'll have to endure trial. Your ministry won't be easy."

Just past Residence Row, Toccoa Creek takes a bend south and to the right. The mobile homes on the small rise across the creek and the cluster of trailers in the heart of "Trailerville" itself all lay right in the path of the maelstrom.

Trailerville really had a more pretentious name, Falls Villa, but somehow that name never stuck to the small community.

As a general residential area for married students at Toccoa Falls College, Trailerville had its own mayor and council. It was a haven of fellowship, a place where a kind of student subculture found its role in the larger college family.

There was a gravel road winding through and trailers were parked in orderly fashion, some newer and some older. The creek, too, passed right through Trailerville. There was also a second level called Upper Trailerville, which was untouched by the flood.

The students visited back and forth. They talked about cars and children. About power tools and trailer skirtings. About sports and term papers.

They talked about the Lord, too. They prayed for each other, loved one another, and baby-sat for each other. They found it tough financially to get through school and also rear their families. "In Trailerville," one of the men recalls, "we were all broke together."

When the flood lurched around the bend in Toccoa Creek there was havoc everywhere and a thousand things happened at once.

Twenty-one were dead or dying—but the voracious flood demanded eighteen more, many of them children. All from Trailerville.

The events at the Jeff Metzgers' were similar to many other homes that fateful November night.

Jeff was working on his campus security detail. The lights were out, so he wasn't able to continue to study or read in the guard shack. Back at his trailer a candle burned.

The guards drove around campus, checking and looking. With no lights to study by, some of the students were out parading around, having fun. The guards stopped and hassled them, also in fun.

Down at the bridge to Trailerville the water-watch was on. The water rose and fell. Some cars were moved and there was idle talk, but no apprehension. And no inkling of what lay ahead.

But at 1:30 a.m. the Metzgers were awakened. People were screaming, "The creek is flooding!"

"So what?" was Jeff's response. But he grabbed a flashlight and as he pulled on his trousers he prayed, "Take us through, Lord."

Suddenly he felt his trailer begin to move. Then he heard a loud bang outside. Metzger dashed into the bedroom, grabbed Dirksen and handed him to his wife Cassie. He picked up Debbie, his little girl, but when he tried to get the door open, he couldn't.

He hit it heavily with his shoulder and it sprang open. As they moved outside, the water was already thigh-deep and rising.

Cassie was making sounds of distress and Metzger couldn't understand why the water was so high.

There was a small creek between Metzger and the safety of the hill just adjacent. The family still had both children. Then Jeff fell into a submerged gully. He scrambled out on the trailer side, still as far away from the bank as ever—and moving dangerously close to the ugly current.

Then Jeff looked back. Nothing! He couldn't believe it. There was water all the way to the far side of the valley! The trailers were gone. He just couldn't believe what he saw.

A car zipped past. Its speed in the water seemed to be at least thirty-five miles per hour. Strangely, though, where the Metzgers were there was no current.

They saw another student, Bob Harner, and tried to walk in his direction. After about twenty feet the current got very swift. The Metzgers tried to go back but couldn't, and in that instant Jeff knew they were in deep trouble.

Then Metzger and his family lost their footing completely. Probably they had walked into the smaller creek that fed the one in the flood.

Jeff, with Debbie in his arms, went under and he knew that Cassie and 2-year-old Dirksen had gone under too.

Metzger vividly remembers fighting and striving to keep hold of his little girl. They were slammed by debris, and Debbie, who was looking over his shoulder, said it was their trailer.

At that point, Jeff felt a tremendous pressure on his chest.

He thought he was going to die right then and hoped the pain would not be too severe.

But the next thing he knew, he was shoved, pushed, and swept toward the bank. There he grabbed the bushes. Somehow he still had hold of Debbie.

Then something big and very heavy settled on his legs. He thought, "Oh no, I've come this far only to have my legs cut off!" But just as suddenly the pressure began to ease.

Later Metzger returned to that spot. He found a rock slab about ten feet long, with a big groove in it and fresh marks. He now thinks it may have been tottering back and forth under the water and that for a moment it had pinned him.

When the pressure had released, though he was badly bruised, he tossed Debbie to safety and climbed out himself. She also was severely bruised, apparently where Jeff's fingers and thumb held her in an iron grip.

It was quiet then, and he rejoiced that God had spared his life. But both father and daughter knew that the rest of the family had been lost.

Then he heard screaming from a grove of trees out in the current. Metzger charged back into the churning water from which he had just emerged, and swam out across the current to where 10-year-old Kendra Smith was perched. A sturdy, strong girl, she was unclothed and screeching like a jaybird.

Jeff grabbed a mattress that had jammed nearby. Then he crossed the current again, pushing the mattress and Kendra to safety.

Jeff recalls the time when Dirksen had been dedicated to God in a church ceremony. Cassie had agonized. She had cried and cried, but finally she had surrendered him to the Lord.

"God must have wanted Dirksen for some reason," Metzger continues. "I think God took Cassie because she couldn't have lived without him. And God never allows us to suffer more than we are able to bear. I think that is why He took Cassie too.

"Debbie and I can stand it. So what if we are left behind? We haven't asked why. We haven't cared why. God has His purposes."

So do not be ashamed to testify about our Lord . . .
but join me in suffering for the gospel, by the
power of God, who has saved us and called us to a
holy life—not because of anything we have done
but because of His own purpose and grace.

2 Timothy 1:8-9

CHAPTER 13

I WANT TO DIE
IN AMERICA

The man in the cockpit of the bomber was new and something had gone wrong. Frantically he pushed buttons—including one that released the bombs.

The high explosives tumbled out onto the tarmac in Thailand.

But they did not explode. If they had, Bob Harner, 25, who was working nearby, would not have lived to come to Toccoa Falls College.

But he was here; and before the flood he had a Thai wife, Tiep, 22, and a baby boy, Robbie, 2.

When he met Tiep she was a slave in Thailand. The Thai didn't like him to say that, but, since she had been bought and sold for money, in his eyes she was a slave. He took her to the Thai police and liberated her; five months later he married her. He had also learned to speak Thai.

Bob and Tiep didn't love each other before they were married, but they knew that love is learned, and Bob believes that they achieved it.

When Tiep came to America she was especially impressed by

the beautifully kept cemeteries. Apparently in Thailand they are not as well kept, and Tiep had said, "I want to die in America."

Since there were no lights the night of the flood, Bob and Tiep had gone to bed early. Tiep's wish was about to come true.

Just before the flood descended upon them in all its force, Bob and Tiep heard screams—"Get out! Get out!" There were also car horns blowing, and Bob immediately figured, "Flash flood!" But by the time he had shaken Tiep four or five times, the water was already moving the trailer off its blocks. When the water hit the trailer, both Robbie and Tiep screamed, but he managed to calm them.

Harner didn't want to stay in the trailer because he saw that other trailers were breaking up. He noticed that Jeff Metzger, another college student, and his wife Cassie were holding their children and making their way toward the mountain. Apparently they had forgotten about the deep ditch right by the bank. The Metzgers did not respond to Harner's warning cry. Then suddenly, they were swept away. Bob missed an outstretched hand by six inches. It might have been Cassie's last desperate grasp for life.

Outside their trailer, Bob and his family clung to the top of a car, but then a backwash of some kind swept them off—Robbie and Tiep one way and Bob another. He never saw them alive again.

For a few moments the violent water tossed Harner between the trailer and the car. Then, somehow, it swept him through a hole that had been punched in the mobile home.

The current sucked him down and kept him there. He was being dragged along the bottom. Three times he planted his feet and tied to leap to the surface. Once he felt nails puncture his feet like a knife slices into an orange. But it didn't hurt, and as he kept trying to swim, passages of David's Psalms raced through his mind. David had cried for deliverance long, long ago and Harner needed deliverance now.

Bob had been converted to Christ as a boy of twelve, then had wandered from his faith while in Thailand. But when Robbie had "died" at birth and then had been revived by cardiac resuscitation, Bob's heart had turned back toward the Lord.

When his lungs were nearly bursting, something pulled Bob upward. He doesn't know what or who it was. When a floating, bobbing car came by, he seized it and it carried him to the old farm where he scrambled out of the water.

"I knew Robbie was gone and the thought came to me, 'Suffer little children to come unto me, and forbid them not.'"

Bob felt that he and his family came to Toccoa Falls College in the will of God. The remarkable manner in which they sold their house for twice the price they paid for it seemed a strong indication of God's direction.

Early that fateful morning, Robbie's body was found. But Bob kept asking for Tiep. Although someone told him she was okay, he felt uncertainty. Later he went to Stephens County Hospital to identify Robbie's body. When he pulled back the sheet to identify Robbie's body, Tiep's body was there too.

Bob had been a member of one of the small clusters of survivors that had emerged on the south side of the floodplain. "The thing we did up there was praise God," he recalls. He especially remembers singing the chorus "God is So Good," and sometimes he sings it now, with tears.

Harner is thoughtful and philosophical about his loss. "Really, I didn't lose anything," he says. "My greatest responsibility as a husband was to see my family come to faith in Christ. My family knew Jesus. They are with the Lord.

"My concept of heaven is different now. Death used to be a place, now it is a door. I now see heaven as a place for worship, not a school in which God will answer questions.

"There was love in Trailerville. I remember Tiep looking for something special to give to Cassie Metzger, our neighbor. The memories still hurt."

Despite the memories, Bob continued classes. He moved into the men's dorm, where he had a roommate who was gradually losing his sight.

The roommates found strength in one another and Harner affirmed, "We have a great relationship.

"Of course," he adds softly, "my roommate now is not as good as the one I had."

In my Father's house are many rooms;
if it were not so, I would have told you.
I am going there to prepare a place for you.

JOHN 14:2

CHAPTER 14

MOMMA STARTS TO PRAY

Mike and Ruth Ann Moore had bought a new bed Saturday, November 5. They had been to town and splurged. That night they stayed up till nearly midnight visiting their neighbors.

But just before 1:30 a.m., somehow sensing that something was wrong, the Moores and Ruth's sister, Donna Porter, a guest in their home, all got up. Baby Jeremiah was in the trailer's addition. The new bed had been used only an hour and a half.

When the Moores looked out they saw about six inches of water on the ground. They got Jeremiah and headed together into Mike's study.

Suddenly the front of the trailer was torn away and what was left was spun around. They could see a massive wall of water coming. It was ten feet over the large bus sitting a few yards away, and it slammed their mobile home into a clump of trees. Then something smashed them from behind.

Mike says, "We were thrown into the water. I was never on top. It seemed that I was under all the time. I came up twice and I tried to swim. I was very scared and I don't think I was ready to die. I tried to stay alive because I didn't know if Ruth and Jeremiah had made it." The water carried Moore nearly a quarter of a mile toward the bridge over Route 17.

Once out on the highway, Mike somehow knew that Ruth and Jeremiah had been lost. "Had I known they were both gone," he says, "I probably would have given up. They seemed to be first in my life, not the Lord.

"But there's been such a change since. Now I would be ready to die.

"God allowed the flood," says Mike. "The devil wanted it done, but now he wishes it had not happened. God has been getting praise and love and glory."

When Mike was thrown into the water, Ruth Ann, Jeremiah, and Donna were somehow held back. Suddenly they too were swept away. They got to a log where Donna and Ruth sought to give mouth-to-mouth resuscitation to the baby. Donna started to take Jeremiah when Ruth said, "No, give him back to me, we're going home to be with Jesus."

Suddenly both Ruth and Jeremiah were sucked under the water. Gone.

Mike continues, "Ruth had grown so much spiritually in the past year. She knew more. She was more ready. I don't think I could have reared Jeremiah. But now I know that he's taken care of.

"It's hard. I want them back, but I have to go on.

"Ruth had prayed so hard that her family would find the Lord. After the tragedy, I went to visit them.

"I drove into their driveway and I just walked into their house. I found Momma sitting on a chair and I simply said, 'You know what you have to do.'

"'Show me how to pray,' she answered. Ruth's mother came to the Lord that day, and Momma's life has been different ever since. There have been others who have turned to the Lord too."

Mike Moore was broken and hurting. He was not one of the

radiant ones after his loss. But he coped. He wept. And as he told me his story, I wanted to weep too.

> *... the Lord gave, and the Lord has taken away;*
> *blessed be the name of the Lord.*
>
> JOB 1:21

CHAPTER 15

IMPALED BY A PLANK

When Mrs. Bea Rupp regained consciousness, she was a quarter of a mile downstream—pinned down by a roof, and with a two-by-four nailed into her thigh. The pain was excruciating; but when she tried to escape from under the roof, the plank kept her impaled.

Fortunately, the water there was shallow and quiet. As she lay there helplessly, she could hear the screams of adults and children and the whining of dogs.

Earlier that evening Mrs. Rupp and her husband Monroe, a retired minister, had gone to bed to a background of sounds far different. Heavy rain had been beating against their trailer roof for three days. But since their home was located on a bank above the creek, they were unconcerned.

"At 8:00 p.m.," says Mrs. Rupp, "the lights went out, so I found a small hurricane lamp and a larger oil lamp. We felt quite cozy, though the lamps did not provide enough light for us to read from our Bible as we usually did. Instead, we quoted some of the chapters we had memorized. Then we sang together.

"My choice was to sing the chorus that ends with the words, 'Sing Hosanna to the King of Kings.' Monroe chose to sing, 'O How I Love Jesus.' After a time of prayer we went to bed.

"At 1:30 a.m. we were suddenly awakened. We jumped out of bed and rushed to the back door. The sight we saw was horrifying! Ralls Hall was afloat and speeding down the swollen creek, and behind the dorm was a wall of water thirty to forty feet high. Immediately we knew the dam above the campus had broken.

"Monroe said, 'Quickly, close the window.' Then he took my hand and rushed toward the front door; but even as we ran down the hall, the water reached our ankles. From then on, everything happened very quickly. It was already too late to escape as the huge wave came upon us.

"The last thing I heard my husband say was, 'Hang onto me.' As we clung to one another, I felt the tremendous force of water hit and break our mobile home to pieces. Then I lost consciousness."

After regaining consciousness, while still impaled by the plank, Mrs. Rupp began to pray audibly and to call for help. She kept it up for three hours. During that time she heard something upstream dislodge and she knew it would once again set the debris moving. "I felt certain I'd be crushed against the roof holding me down," she said. "But then I sensed a voice within me say, 'Move to the right.'

"I knew I had to obey that inner voice, so I squirmed my shoulders over as far as possible, still pinned down by the plank. The debris came crashing down past my left side."

Bea Rupp, struggling with pain and nearly immersed in stinking water, had no choice but to wait.

"Finally, after three hours in the cold waters, one of our students found me and sat with me until rescue workers came. In the darkness he had heard my voice and came to me.

"My husband went home to be with Jesus that early morning.

The parting has been extremely hard, but I'm reminded of the first verse of our wedding song:

All the way my Savior leads me,
What have I to ask beside?
Can I doubt His tender mercy,
Who thro' life has been my Guide?
Heav'nly peace, divinest comfort,
Here by faith in Him to dwell!
For I know, what e'er befall me,
Jesus doeth all things well.

"ALL THE WAY MY SAVIOR LEADS ME"
© PUBLIC DOMAIN. AUTHORS: FANNY JANE CROSBY | ROBERT S. LOWRY

It was a long struggle for Mrs. Rupp. Her wound was badly infected by the polluted water. But four surgeries did not dim Bea Rupp's enthusiasm to do God's will, nor her conviction that He does, indeed, do all things well. She told us over the phone, "The Lord is becoming more and more precious to me."

* * *

"We've been saved four years," said Thurman and Dixie Kemp, who came from Florida. They weren't telling about being rescued from the flood, but they were describing the religious conversion that led them to study at Toccoa Falls College.

"Ours was the first trailer to go, but the five houses were already gone," said Dixie. She was referring to Residence Row.

The Kemp home was set on a little hill above the creek, but certainly not high enough to save them from that fateful morning.

The evening before, all four of the Kemps had gotten into their king-size bed. Chris, just 7, had read a story. Morgan, his brother, 9, had read one too. It had been a beautiful family time.

The spirit had been unusual. Later as Dixie lay in a hospital bed, still not knowing that Thurman and Morgan had survived, she thought, "God gave us a very special time."

Mrs. Ruby Kemp, Thurman's elderly mother, had been a guest in the home and when awakened about 1:30 a.m. she began to scream, "It's a tornado!" Her warning saved the lives of the Kemp family. A non-swimmer, she herself rode a piece of furniture to safety.

When Thurman was aroused, the water was already two feet high on the door. He managed to get to the back of the trailer as Morgan ran to him. Dixie tried to waken Chris, but he seemed to be leaden on his feet.

Suddenly, in the turbine-like thrashing of water and in the reeling movements of their floating trailer, the floor collapsed. Dixie felt Chris being pulled away from her. Twice she pulled him back. But the third time he slipped out of her grasp. "I think now," she said, "that Chris was already gone. He felt so heavy."

"I must have been hit, I 'came to' underwater. But there was nothing beautiful about it like I had heard it was supposed to be when a person enters heaven.

"Come on, Lord," she prayed, "where's the beauty?"

Then she was struck on the head and temporarily lost sight in one eye. "Lord," she prayed, "drown me or get me out of this—but do it quick!"

Coming to the surface, Mrs. Kemp looked to the left. Through the debris there was a little path. She climbed out.

"I think an angel pushed me out," she said. "Then I thought about my family. How could I live without them? I thought about jumping back in."

But a phrase from the Scriptures slipped into her mind: "beauty for ashes." And later Mrs. Kemp said, "The Lord gave me just that."

Dixie Kemp was the first of her family to the hospital. She'd had the quickest trip.

Thurman and Morgan had been pulled in another direction. They were moving, Kemp feels, in excess of thirty-five miles per hour.

"We were swept up against a hill where an undertow pulled us apart. Then I grabbed a tree, turned around, and I saw Morgan again. Instantly I grabbed him. It was a miracle that I turned around when I did, and that he was right there.

"We clambered out onto the hillside and then climbed higher. Morgan had a big hole in his leg, but it didn't bleed. He didn't get scared, and he didn't cry for three and a half hours."

"By 5 a.m. we knew that Chris was gone," the Kemps stated. At 9:00 a.m. his body was identified.

Despite their loss and the grief they felt, both Thurman and Dixie cooperated with the probing newsmen. One questioned Thurman about the earthen dam that had taken his son and so many of his friends.

He replied, "If God had wanted to hold that dam together He could have done it with a Band-Aid."

When another reporter asked him how he coped with the tragic situation, he answered, along with the New Testament: "In all things God works for the good of those who love Him, who have been called according to His purpose."

The day that Chris was buried, an aunt and an uncle, who had travelled to the funeral in separate cars, both declared that they too had placed their trust in Jesus Christ. The death of a little boy had drawn them into the fold.

Dixie concludes, "My little boy's funeral was full of grace and glory . . . I really feel that those lives that were taken were an offering to God, a sweet-smelling sacrifice to redeem the school and to reach out to the world.

"I think that God is trying to say, 'Hey, world, wake up, I love you.'"

We have a feeling that Dixie Kemp's conclusion is exactly right.

> *This precious value, then, is for you who believe ....*
>
> 1 Peter 2:7

GET OUT! GET OUT!

"Get out! Get out! The dam has broken!" It was Denise Woerner running through Trailerville sounding the alarm.

Bill Anderson, 33, a stocky New Englander, fumbled open his trailer window and heard the words clearly. He thought there might be water—but he had no idea how much.

By the time he had pulled on his trousers, his wife had tumbled their five children out of bed and had herded them into the hallway.

Bill explained to his family, "There's a flood!" Then they started to pray, asking God to keep them from panic and to give them strength.

At that point, the trailer began to move. Almost simultaneously a tremendous force slammed against it. Anderson later realized it may have been the big wave.

The roof was torn off and inside there was turmoil—but somehow the Andersons got their children calmed down. And they encouraged them to trust in the Lord.

Because the hallway seemed to be the safest place, Mrs. Anderson and the two youngest children stayed there.

Bill stacked furniture and climbed up to peer out through the slash in the roof.

A second crash came, ripping off the end of the trailer. This time, instead of panicking, the children cried, "Jesus! Jesus!"

Bill observed that they were nearing trees. When their trailer lodged against them, he tossed his oldest daughter, 12-year-old Lisa, and his oldest son, 6-year-old Billy, into the branches of the trees.

Bill's wife Karen stayed in the hallway of the sinking trailer home. Bill heard her say to the children, "Come on, kids, get ready. We're going to meet Jesus." She was getting them prepared.

Clinging to the top of the trailer, Bill turned in time to see the wall collapse inward—right where his wife and two of his children stood. There was a swirl of water and they were gone. Anderson himself was thrown into the water. Desperately he clawed and scrambled over the debris toward the trees—and not once did he get wet above the shoulders.

But he knew his wife and two youngest children were with the Lord. "Thank you, Lord," he prayed, "they don't have to suffer anymore."

But uncertainty about his other daughter Susan persisted. She hadn't been under that wall. He didn't know where she was.

"I did sense the presence of Jesus," he stated. "It seemed as if the Lord had just reached down and taken my wife and children. There was peace that calmed my heart."

Clinging to a tree, with his feet on a wire, Bill Anderson saw flashlight beams. There were people in the woods. Dave Woerner helped the surviving Andersons to the shore, and then he and Bill began to lead other survivors to their group. Because of the nakedness of some of them, they said, "Huddle together. Keep warm. Put your arms around each other and lean against each other."

Then Anderson heard cries.

"Daddy! Daddy!"

It was Susan.

"Is that you, Susie?"

"Yes. Can you help me?"

"Where are you?"

"I'm on a piece of tin."

"Is it a big piece of tin?"

"Yes."

"Is it moving?"

"No."

Anderson ordered his daughter to stay put. And later Susan was rescued from the other side of the swollen creek.

When Anderson's relatives came south from Vermont for the funeral service, Bill took one look at his sister. Somehow she looked different. Soon, in a private moment, she told him, "I've found the Lord."

"I knew it," Anderson responded.

Later when they went for a drive, Bill's older brother said, "I didn't come here for the funeral."

"What's the matter?" said Bill.

"I'm here to see you. I want what you've got." Bill Anderson led his brother to faith in Jesus Christ.

Karen and Bill Anderson had prayed for conversions in Bill's family for years. A Toccoa friend said of Karen, "She had redemption on her mind. She would gladly have died if she thought it would bring others to the Lord."

Asked why there seemed to be serenity in the face of such grievous loss, Bill Anderson said, "The knowledge and certainty in our hearts that these loved ones are with the Lord now and that the Lord is present with us now makes all the difference."

In our interviews with the survivors of the Toccoa Falls College flood, we consistently observed this serenity. Not without tears and sorrow necessarily, but quiet joy.

And we feel obliged to agree with Anderson. This knowledge does make a tremendous difference.

> *... I consider everything a loss compared to the surpassing greatness of knowing Christ Jesus my Lord, for whose sake I have lost all things.*
>
> PHILIPPIANS 3:8

CHAPTER 17

THE BUS
DIDN'T STOP

The old college bus was floating along in the flood tide as Jerry Nicholson and his wife Pat clung to a mattress on which they had placed one of their 7-year-old twin boys. The other twin clutched the mattress too. Jerry looked up and said, "Here comes the bus. I wonder if it'll stop!"

Later he surmised that they could have been "sailed over."

When the flood hit the Nicholson home in Trailerville, Jerry had looked out the door. He noticed the other mobile homes begin to move out into the current like toy boats. Then their own trailer began to drift.

In the darkness Pat began to pray, "Lord Jesus, help us!" Then another mobile home crashed into them, ripping a five-foot gash in their living room.

That gash was a specific answer to their prayers. It was a way out! The Nicholsons began to struggle with a sofa that had kept afloat in the rising water. Suddenly it popped open and a mattress fell out.

As it did, Jerry heard a desperate cry from the water. He saw an arm and a head, apparently a woman in distress, but then she was gone.

Both of the Nicholsons' twin sons had taken swimming lessons. Tim got on the mattress, but Michael seemed to keep falling off. Finally he just seized the foam mattress and held on. Pat and Jerry ended up alongside the mattress, one on each side.

At about that time, the bus came by. It didn't stop!

Once the Nicholsons neared the shore by what is called the old farm road, Archie Smith hauled them out of the water. He was unclad, but they hardly even noticed. He ushered them through a barbed wire fence as he had helped others. Though Archie's back later showed a number of lacerations from where he had held up the wire fence, he didn't seem to notice the pain.

When Archie said, "All my family is gone," Jerry impulsively replied, "We'll be your family."

Jerry, Pat, and the boys joined the group on the hillside, where they found sadness and serenity. There was such a beautiful spirit in the group. There was love and compassion. And even humor.

Somebody said, "That's one way to get a pool in your back yard." The pool's water, they decided, was "sure dirty."

Archie Smith is a big man. Maybe 300 pounds. And everyone was cold. So they all huddled around him. "Come ahead," he invited, "fat is where it's at!" This from a shy man who thought his family had not survived.

But when the news came that Archie's family was safe, everyone rejoiced together.

The humor, though surprising, broke the tension and proved helpful. There was no mistaking Jerry and Pat Nicholson's seriousness. They believed that God saved their family in a remarkable way and were very grateful.

They believed the Scripture which says, ". . . give thanks in all circumstances, for this is God's will for you in Christ Jesus." (1 Thessalonians 5:18). And they believed like the rest of the people in Trailerville that it should be practiced.

Archie Smith was another who believed it.

The water caught the Smiths on the floodplain fleeing toward Upper Trailerville. Archie saw they weren't going to make it, so he grabbed an exposed sewer pipe.

He submerged, but when he came up he was inexplicably right beside a student's car. He grabbed the bumper and floated to safety—in the area of the old farm. Strangely, he remembered that the taillights were on.

When he got to a tree, the car stopped, so he seized the tree and the car promptly sank. Later he scrambled to safety.

According to one report, twenty-seven trailers were swept away. The next day, in front of the few that remained, fragile flowers still danced in the breeze.

A note in a young boy's handwriting carried a request to be awakened on the next day. It also said, "I love you, Mom."

A dog named Rufus made his own escape. Chained to his doghouse, he just pulled it up the incline.

Actually, in Trailerville there are many more powerful accounts.

Mercifully, the waters moved on toward the concrete bridge over Route 17.

It held. Had it not, the toll would have mounted down-stream. But because the bridge over Route 17 held, it became a secondary dam which sent a wall of water in reverse—a final stroke on the shattered remains of Trailerville.

…the prayer of a righteous man is powerful and effective.

JAMES 5:16

CHAPTER 18

WE SWIMMED AND SWIMMED

There is one more painful spot in Trailerville. Bill Ehrensberger's house, where only one person survived.

Bill had already been pulled off his feet and was gone.

Eldon Elsberry stared at Ehrensberger's home as it began to float away, but he was powerless to save Peggy Ehrensberger and her four children, even though his own ordeal was past.

But Tommy, one of the small boys, did survive. Robert, Kristin, and Kenny were swept away with their mother.

All we know is that little Tommy was thrown into the water and that at one point he had hold of his older brother Robbie's hand.

"We swimmed and swimmed," said Tommy, pathetically.

Apparently, he climbed onto a log only to be knocked off. Finally, Doug Veer, who had barely survived himself, pulled Tommy from the water.

While he waited for news about his family, Tommy was enveloped with the love and concern of one of the groups of survivors on the south shore of Toccoa Creek. They held him close and kept him warm.

When he asked about his mommy and daddy and wondered when they were coming for him, Tommy was told that his parents were missing and that no one knew where they were.

Tommy's stoic reply was, "That's okay."

Later he asked where Robbie was. But when told, "He's gone, too," Tommy said, "Well, I thought so with all this water."

Tommy ended up moving in with Peggy's parents in St. Mary's, Pennsylvania. He was wrapped in love with Bill's parents also living nearby.

The dramatic last moments in a reeling, tilting home are unknown. The entrance that Peggy and her three children had into God's presence cannot be described till we see at last through the veil that clouds our vision from this world to the next.

The story we can't tell is what happened when the heavens opened. And surely they opened wide at 1:30 a.m. that dark November morning.

Within thirty seconds many of the Toccoa Falls College victims were already in.

Stephen, who went in centuries before them and whose words are recorded in the Bible, said as he was about to cross over, "Behold, I see the heavens opened and the Son of Man standing at the right hand of God."

What those who entered from the flood saw we cannot tell. But Whom they saw we know. Some of us who read (and write) these lines find these witnesses and their words almost too powerful. Clearly, these people "sorrow not as others who have no hope."

What splendor and power would fill these pages if we could load this text with explosive details from the life that is "far better."

Impossible, of course. But mark it well. There is a heavenly side to this Toccoa Falls College story. Incredible. Intense. And full of gripping detail.

One day, most certainly, that story will be told.

...No eye has seen, no ear has heard, no mind has conceived what God has prepared for those who love him—but God has revealed it to us by his Spirit.

1 CORINTHIANS 2:9-10

IV. OUT OF THE VALLEY

CHAPTER 19

TWELVE HELICOPTERS ON THE LAWN

There was that sound.

Then that door.

Then that stretcher. And Ken Sanders, then basketball coach of the Toccoa Falls Eagles, knew that death was there again.

Advised of the dam break by one of his players, Tom Penland, Sanders had descended from his home on higher ground to the campus at about 2:30 a.m.

He found no panic, only silence and a stench he had never smelled before. As Dean of Student Services, Sanders felt an immediate concern for Dave Eby and his family. (Eby served under him as Dean of Men.) For that reason, he moved toward the still-angry stream.

Then there was a cry across the creek where Eby's house once had stood.

"Dave?" said Sanders.

"Who is it?" the voice responded.

"Sanders. It that you, Dave?"

It was. He and his family were all safe. Eby slid across the swollen creek on a fallen tree, and the men embraced and wept. Blood from a wound on Eby's arm seeped through Sanders' shirt.

But death was in the air. They hoped and prayed there wouldn't be more victims—but they were afraid there might be.

They headed for the hospital to see the injured and anxious. Death they had left behind. Or so they thought.

Then there was a sound. The turning of a knob. The opening of a door. Then down the hall came a stretcher and death was there again. They had not left it at all. Sanders was asked to stay and help identify the dead. He stayed and did exactly that.

"I cried those fifteen hours," said Sanders, "seeing some I loved, some I knew, and others I would had loved if I had known them.

"The hurt came most when the hospital looked clear and then there was that sound, and then that door, and then that stretcher, and I knew that death was there again.

"The room filled up again with friends and I cried, 'When will it end?'"

At 6:00 p.m., two were still missing, and darkness fell over Toccoa Falls College. Sanders went home.

Stephens County Hospital, a solid brick building surrounded by spacious lawns, sits on land deeded to it by the College.

It is also close to the bridge across Toccoa Creek that allows Georgia's Route 17 to roll into the City of Toccoa. All the victims were swept in that direction and those that could headed directly for the hospital.

The scenes at the hospital will never be forgotten. Some victims arrived who were unrecognizable because of injuries. There was a father who followed stretcher after stretcher into the morgue—till he found what he hoped he wouldn't find.

Ruth Payton, a registered nurse, helped Sanders and David Wilson, a student, identify many of the bodies. She knew most of the victims personally and prayed before each identification, "Lord, help me to remember that whoever this is, I am just identifying the shell that once housed the person and he or she is already rejoicing in your presence."

The bodies of the families were kept together in the morgue.

At about 10:00 a.m. the Governor of Georgia, George Busbee, and his entourage arrived. The army was coming in too. Later Senator Herman E. Talmadge and Congressman Ed Jenkins also visited the campus. Busbee was present when the bodies of three children were pulled from the carnage in the creek.

A decision had been made earlier to take the bodies to the two funeral homes in Toccoa where they were embalmed. Some of the bodies were later shifted between mortuaries according to family preference.

After the bodies were embalmed they were taken to a temporary morgue in an elementary school gymnasium in Toccoa.

Both the Governor and the Commander of the National Guard operated out of the hospital complex. Governor Busbee told Hospital Administrator J. W. Warren that U.S. President Jimmy Carter's wife Rosalynn was coming. Shortly after, her secret service detail arrived.

Warren, the Governor, and Kenn Opperman all greeted Mrs. Carter. She had flown to the Anderson Air Force Base in South Carolina and then had been driven over the state line into Georgia.

The media also made the hospital a focal point, and at one time there were a dozen helicopters on the manicured lawn.

America's gracious First Lady visited Jeff Metzger first. Jeff knew that his wife and son were dead. But despite his pain, he was cheerful.

Mrs. Carter also visited others who had lost loved ones or been injured. She found a similar phenomenon.

At one point she is reported to have said, "I came down here to help and give what little comfort I could to the victims and their families, but I feel I'm taking away more than I'm able to give."

There were some unusual mental health aspects to the disaster. At one time, Warren believed there were between 150 to 200 students jammed into the halls and doorways. But generally there were no "hangups" and very little hysteria. There was, instead, a general acceptance of God's will.

The bodies of children brought the tears. The second body brought in was that of a child. Pathetically, one little child's hand held a stick. Warren, a hospital administrator of twenty-nine years experience, admitted that the sight of that little victim broke him up. He had a daughter about the same age.

The events at the hospital also had a spiritual impact on Warren. In his own words he said, "My faith was deepened." He had been a churchman all his life, but he gained "inside knowledge" during the disaster's aftermath.

Dr. John Payton, formerly an Alliance missionary to Thailand, greeted the ambulance driver when he arrived at Stephens County Hospital Monday morning. "Theo, thank you for being so good to our people," he said.

The driver replied, "Dr. Payton, those people were easy to care for. We've had more hysteria at a two-car collision than we had all that night and the next morning!"

Another hospital official, when questioned, told Payton, "I am sure there must have been some hysteria among the younger students last night, but we saw none."

When Payton checked the records for the night, only one shot of valium had been given and only one shot of narcotics had been administered to the victims.

The one girl who did become hysterical had been on a date just the night before with one of the fellows who had drowned in the dorm.

The local mental health officials, understanding the unique nature of the Toccoa Falls College community, knew that extensive mental health counseling would not be needed.

Not everyone understood, though. At one point, a Washington-based mental health official insisted on seeking out victims who needed psychological counseling. And she wasn't too happy to discover that there was little need for her services.

When the message was relayed to Dr. Payton, he responded, "We have about five hundred of the most accommodating people in the world out there at the college. If she needs victims, I'm sure we can find some volunteers!"

A thoughtful man, John Payton cited two main reasons for the scarcity of severe mental stress.

"Among evangelical people there is the practice of child dedication," he said. "Parents formally present their children to God for Him to enact His will in their lives. Later—if the children should die—parents find death easier to accept. They have already given those children to God.

"Secondly, in the case of Toccoa Falls College, Dr. Jerry Sproull had exerted a considerable influence on the young couples' marital relationships. He had encouraged the couples to always deal with conflicts immediately, to resolve all strife, and thus to fulfill the biblical injunction, 'Do not the sun go down while you are still angry.'"

The wounded did weep and bleed, of course, the morning of November 6 in the Stephens County Hospital. But in that, too, there was strength, serenity, and power.

W. A. "Bill" Warren summed it up for everyone when he told a reporter, "If you can capture what we saw here at the hospital, people will be knocking down the doors to get into this College."

But for Coach Sanders, the trauma was not over. On December 3, nearly a month after the disaster, a student came to Sanders at the College Christmas banquet. Again, it was a basketball player, Jon Penland. He was concerned that one of the students had not arrived. Soon it was learned that there had been an accident. Two cars had collided and Mrs. Bertha Walls, the youthful wife of a young man who had replaced Betty Jean Woerner as Dr. Opperman's secretary, had been injured.

After he learned of the accident, Dr. Alvin Moser, the vice president, proceeded to deliver his address.

Its theme: though Bethlehem was small and obscure, God chose to make it widely known as a place of joy and blessing where multitudes return figuratively every Christmas to find hope and peace. In a similar fashion, God has been pleased to make obscure Toccoa Falls College a symbol of this same hope and peace to the world.

Then once more Ken Sanders and Alvin Moser headed for the Stephens County Hospital. And one last time they stared death in the face. Bertha Walls was gone too. Death had visited the College yet another time.

Finally, the hand of death was stayed at Toccoa Falls College. And life, warm as the breath of spring, blew across campus. The ordeal by accidents and flood was past. A new day dawned.

It doesn't matter anymore that Toccoa Falls College had been in difficult financial straits before the flood. Nor was any credence given to the rumors that said the college could never survive. The old school that served so well for so long was not going to die after all.

She really is the "planting of the Lord."

Forget the former things; do not dwell
on the past. See, I am doing a new thing!
now it springs up; do you not perceive it?

Isaiah 43:18-19a

CHAPTER 20

STABILITY COMES THROUGH

"Dad, the whole campus is washing away!"

Dr. Kenn Opperman, president of Toccoa Falls College, was awakened in Florida by a call from his son Bob at home on campus.

Over the phone, as an awesome background to his son's voice, Opperman heard the snapping of timbers and the roar of water four-tenths of a mile away. But he could not be there to help.

Dr. Alvin Moser, vice president of the college, was the highest administrative official on the grounds. It fell to him to gather the students and to lead and encourage them.

The college was in shock and stability and calmness were needed.

Moser prayed for daylight.

When the water first began to rampage through the lower campus, the several hundred students and other college personnel were uncertain as to where it would go or how much water would come. The dormitories emptied and students milled around. Vehicles seeking to negotiate the campus roads found their way blocked by anxious students gathered in little clusters. The students prayed. There was weeping and great distress. And a thousand times the questions were asked, "Where is . . . ?" "Have you seen . . . ?"

Ironically, there were others who slept through the whole night. They did not know until the next morning that the dam had broken.

In a service conducted by Dr. Moser at 10:00 a.m. in the chapel, the students offered testimonies and requested prayers. Songs were chosen and sung. The stability of the Christian faith was coming through.

Stayed upon Jehovah,
Hearts are fully blessed,
Finding as He promised,
Perfect peace and rest.

"Like A River Glorious" © Public Domain
Authors: Frances Ridley Havergal | James Mountain

The flow of rumors ebbed and rose.

By that time the news media had arrived and the students' reactions were being chronicled for distribution across the nation and the world.

Apparently, too, the newsmen were not prepared for the openness and guilelessness of the students. Some reporters, who followed disasters regularly, had never encountered reactions like they found at Toccoa Falls College.

College personnel were also vigorous in their witness. They spoke simply about the disaster and about their faith in Jesus Christ. When one student asked Mrs. May Trucano, editor of the College quarterly *TFC Today*, when the reporters would leave, Mrs. Trucano's answer was precise—"They will go when God is through with them."

The attitude toward death, the spontaneity and the joy among the students of the college were striking to the world outside, but Vice President Moser believed the disaster only illuminated what was present in their lives all the time. Undoubtedly he was right.

It must be said, too, that not was all joy and peace. There was heaviness, and hurt, and tears.

Some of the students wondered if the college would be able to survive. On Sunday morning a meeting was convened in the chapel and a number of announcements were made.

One of the first was made by Mr. J. J. Fowler of Atlanta, chairman of the Board of Trustees. "This is not the end of Toccoa Falls College," he said. "It's just a new beginning."

Immediately there was a thundering emotional response from the audience. Sustained clapping and applause. A standing ovation. Below the open concern for loved ones and friends, apparently there had been a deep anxiety about the future of the college itself.

Photographers and reporters in the back of the auditorium could hardly believe what they were witnessing. The father of one of the students, overcome by emotion, slipped out of the hall to pray. He wanted desperately to get right with God.

By 5:00 that afternoon, the campus dormitories had been vacated. Most had returned to their homes. Others had gone to stay at the Georgia Baptist Conference Center at nearby Lake Louise in Stephens County.

In the days that followed, the Civil Defense under General Billy Jones carried out a massive cleanup that quickly erased most of the signs of the flood.

The offers of help came from all over America. Sometimes there were so many offers that there was no way to cope with them.

Inmates from a nearby correctional institution, some of whom had been led to Christ by students, volunteered their services. At one point down near the floodplain, the inmates offered to help load some cattle into a truck. One of the animals bolted and more than twenty inmates in hot pursuit followed it over the hill.

The dumbfounded guard was heard to say, "This could be trouble!"

But they all came back. And later they caught the animal too.

The day of the Memorial Service, held November 16 at 8:00 a.m. in the Student Center, was a memorable one.

Heavy showers preceded the gathering and a magnificent double rainbow hovered over the campus. Many saw it as a symbol of beauty and hope for broken hearts. It also seemed to say, "Toccoa Falls College will never be destroyed by flood again."

The service was simple and full of deep dignity.

There were expressions of thanks, majestic music, and a healing message of optimism by President Opperman.

He said, "For those who can't quite comprehend the great victory, the smiling faces, the victorious statements—for those who say, 'How can this possibly be?'—the answer is found in the nature of the family that is drawn together at Toccoa Falls College. It's made up of young men and women from around the world who need His strength, who have had an encounter with Him, who know that they don't have to return but that they to have to go—and so, to the best of their ability, they're training to go.

"Many worldwide organizations have sent us letters and communications offering us aid—and for all such help I am indeed grateful—but some of the deepest feelings of my heart have been for people who lost everything . . . house, accumulations, furniture . . . everything. In two cases, married students who had nothing left on this earth went to the bank and withdrew every penny of their savings. Instead of saying, 'I've got to survive,' they came to me with their checks and said 'Toccoa Falls College must survive!'

"How can you explain that kind of dedication?

"Sixty-four years ago when Dr. R. A. Forrest sat on a stone with a stick in his hand, almost absentmindedly working his way through the ashes of what had once been Haddock Inn, the first home of Toccoa Falls College, he sat there with tears running down his cheeks. Then he heard a voice speak to him from heaven. And as the Lord drew near to him, He seemed to say, 'Weep not, for you shall have beauty for ashes. Do you not know? This school is the planting of the Lord. It shall continue.'

"Our young people recognize that life is filled with trouble," he continued. "Yet I find among these Christian youth a radiance, an acceptance of God's will, an awareness that God has done something very beautiful for them.

"Many have asked us, 'What accounts for the radiance of the people here?' I have only one answer, an answer that a person who isn't a Christian can't accept. It's found in the Bible: 'Christ in you, the hope of glory.' For a Christian the most important thing is a relationship with Christ so whether we live or die we glorify the Lord Jesus.

"There's something unusual here at Toccoa. It's found in young people who are already committed to the fact that life is meant to be lived every day and death is not something to be dreaded. We mourn the thirty-nine who are no longer with us, yet we know they are with their Master.

"Toccoa Falls College is going to continue because we believe we need to train men and women to preach the gospel of Jesus Christ until the King Himself returns. We intend to do that." (*The Alliance Witness*, December 28, 1977.)

... Christ in you, the hope of glory.

Colossians 1:27

CHAPTER 21

DISASTER WITH A DIFFERENCE

The coordinator for all agencies of the U.S. government in the Toccoa Falls College disaster was hunched behind the chair in front of him—praying and crying.

At Toccoa he had found a disaster with a difference—and even in the crowd of 1,500 that had gathered in the Student Center at 8:00 a.m. November 16 for the Memorial Service, he had been unable to escape its personal implications.

Tom Credle, 53, from Atlanta, was not a man easily moved to tears. But at Toccoa Falls College, the disaster coordinator for the U.S. government, a veteran of nineteen previous disasters, a pragmatic man with military background, found himself strangely overwhelmed with emotional and spiritual concern.

He had sought out the chair at the rear of the auditorium because as the "field fed," the top governmental official on the scene, Credle had a feeling that Dr. Opperman might call upon him for a few words. And he considered himself in no shape for words of any kind.

Kenn Opperman said to him after the service, "Where were

you? I was going to call on you." Credle's "feeling" had been well founded!

Tom Credle had heard about the flood at Toccoa Falls College the morning of November 6. He was on the scene early in the day, and his first impressions were not unusual at all. It was another disaster with the usual debris and suffering. But as one of the ten federal disaster coordinators in the country, he was responsible to set up an office and to coordinate work in the area until the cleanup and repairs had been accomplished. He returned to Atlanta to prepare a summary of his findings.

When a decision had to be made at Credle's office about whom to send, Tom Credle chose to go himself.

It was a casual decision—that ultimately proved to be momentous.

Once on the campus, Credle soon observed that his relationship with God seemed anemic when compared with that of the students and faculty at Toccoa Falls.

Also, uncomfortably, a question began to hammer his mind—"Why did this happen to Toccoa Falls College?"

Never in any other disaster had he become personally involved. Never had he had any questions. But now there was an overpowering concern. So overpowering, in fact, that it drove him to his knees in his Toccoa motel.

Why had this happened to Toccoa Falls College? Why? Why? "Maybe, Lord, You can tell me why," he prayed.

Part of that answer came soon—back on the campus. Credle didn't realize that capable graduates from Toccoa Falls College were actively engaged in full-time Christian service in fifty-six countries of the world and in all fifty states. No matter. Credle's conclusion was clear. "Toccoa Falls College and the mission that it has must continue."

Tom Credle also knew that the college had been in a desperate situation financially even before the flood. And he realized that the dramatic events had suddenly pushed Toccoa Falls College into national focus. At the price of thirty-nine lives, it had been thrust into the national consciousness. Undoubtedly, Toccoa Falls College had become, overnight, the best-known small college in the United States. The response of the U.S. government had something very vital to do with the college's survival.

Tom Credle's personal spiritual odyssey was far from over. During subsequent days on campus he frequented Dr. Opperman's office, and not just to iron out details or procedures. He went, he says, to draw strength. To talk and to pray.

In private moments he noticed, too, that his knees were more limber than they had been in the past. It was easier to pray. More comfortable in God's presence. His questions, however, were only partly answered.

But as Jimmy Carter's man on the scene drove toward the Student Center for that early-morning Memorial Service, the second part of his private puzzle fell into place.

A massive, richly colored rainbow arched upward into the sky over the campus. He was awestruck—so much so that he asked others if they had seen what he had seen. They had. And its message was clear.

Toccoa Falls College would continue. God would see to that. God knew what He was doing at Toccoa.

And now Credle knew it too.

I have placed my rainbow in the clouds. It is the sign of my covenant with you and with all the earth.... I will remember my covenant with you and with all living creatures. Never again will the floodwaters destroy all life.

GENESIS 9:13, 15 NLT

CHAPTER 22

WHY THIS RESPONSE?

A visiting reporter on the campus of Toccoa Falls College asked Professor Gerald E. McGraw how he was ever going to vindicate God in the eyes of his students after such a great disaster.

McGraw, a tall theologian, moved and spoke very deliberately. His reply in this case was very careful.

"The question has never even come up," he said honestly.

To a reporter unschooled in biblical ideas, Dr. McGraw's reply was stunning. We are sure his reply will also puzzle some who read this book. But then, his response is just one more of the highly unusual reactions chronicled between these covers.

Frankly, there is no possibility of understanding a book like this without first understanding the responses that came from minds and hearts steeped in the Bible and determined to obey its teachings.

Toccoa Falls College is a *Christian* institution, and there was clearly a theological response to the flood at Toccoa Falls College. The Scriptures teach that God is sovereign, above all, and ultimately in control. Perhaps for that reason the text summoned most often by these people in the midst of their disaster was this one: "And we know that in all things God works for the good of those who love him, who have been called according to His purpose." (Romans 8:28).

This perspective is the real explanation for the relative serenity that prevailed on the ravaged campus at Toccoa Falls College.

Why did President Opperman reach back into history to use such phrases as "beauty for ashes" and "the planting of the Lord" (Isaiah 61:3)? He believed, as did the whole community, that the Bible is without error, inspired, alive, eternal, and completely trustworthy. That's why words written by the prophet Isaiah or by King David thousands of years ago are considered helpful and encouraging today. "All Scripture," Opperman would say with Saint Paul, "is God-breathed, and is useful for teaching, rebuking, correcting and training in righteousness" (2 Timothy 3:16).

Reporters did not expect to find verifying evidence of the truth of Christianity on the Toccoa Falls College campus. But expected or not, it was there.

Actually, there was no escaping it. The whole college community demonstrated a deep, personal knowledge of Jesus Christ. That's why Dr. Alvin Moser affirmed that the disaster only illuminated what was present all the time in the lives of the students. That is why Dr. John Payton told us, "Now I really know that what I've been telling others about Jesus is true."

Surprisingly, the flood supplied hard evidence, and plenty of it, that Jesus Christ is alive.

The thanksgiving in difficult straits is also nearly impossible to understand unless one is governed by the biblical principle, "give thanks in all circumstances" (1 Thessalonians 5:18).

That's a high order. You may have been amazed that a little boy locked in an air bubble in a truck cab actually did it. Perhaps you were puzzled when a young widow, just bereaved, found strength to do it. Clearly, the Bible drastically alters human behavior.

Ordinarily, in disasters such as the one at Toccoa Falls College, there are all kinds of threats, recriminations, and words of anger. They just were not heard at Toccoa Falls College. Somehow the reactions of these people of the Book were different.

The way they faced death was different too. There was strength, serenity, calmness. It seems that believers who have invited Jesus Christ to be their Lord and Savior somehow know, intuitively and deeply, that they have eternal life. Death is neither welcomed nor sought by them, of course. But the dread is gone. Death, for them has lost its sting. "Where, O death, is your victory? Where, O death, is your sting?" (1 Corinthians 15:55). With the Apostle Paul they say, "... absent from the body ... present with the Lord" (2 Corinthians 5:8). There is a whole philosophy of death and dying in these pages that can only be explained by the Scriptures.

At Toccoa Falls College these biblical ideas were like the rails that carried the trains through storms and darkness. They provided stability and direction. Death simply did not threaten these people the way it threatens casual Christians or unbelieving humanists. Christians have always died well, and they always will.

In the next chapter you will read a letter from a man who was watching a television newscast. And we'll tell you this much now, as he watched the reaction at Toccoa Falls College, he was converted to faith in Jesus Christ. The same thing happened to him that happened to Bill Anderson's brother pages earlier. (Remember, he didn't come to Toccoa for the funeral, he came to get what Bill had.) The same thing happened repeatedly as people responded to the events at Toccoa Falls College, and it is only partially recorded here.

What is the meaning of all this? Again, it is the application of biblical ideas to life. The man who watched the newscast in which flood survivors told their stories apparently knew some important biblical teachings.

Somewhere he had learned that Jesus Christ died for everyone. "For God so loved the world, that he gave his one and only Son, that whoever believes in him shall not perish, but have eternal life" (John 3:16).

Further, he also obviously accepted the Bible's verdict as applying to himself. ". . . for all have sinned, and fall short of the glory of God" (Romans 3:23). Apparently, he felt a personal need to turn from his sins.

Somewhere he had also heard the biblical concept of personal responsibility. "Yet to all who received him, to those who believed in his name, He gave the right to become the children of God. . . ." (John 1:12). He knew he had to do something. And the witness on the television broadcast pushed him over the line of decision.

Finally, he obviously acted upon what he had known previously, and perhaps what he had felt through the telecast. He called upon the Lord. And it is the Book which says, "Everyone who calls on the name of the Lord will be saved" (Romans 10:13). In biblical terminology, he had been saved, born again.

When he wrote the College, whether he knew it or not, he was acting upon another biblical principle. "For it is with your heart that you believe and are justified, and it is with your mouth that you confess and are saved." (Romans 10:10). Real believers always make it known.

What happened to that believer will happen to some of our readers too. We know that. The accounts in these pages are like bare electric wires. When you seize them, you will feel the power.

We do not object, of course. We're pleased. But we think you should know how it happens and why. God the Holy Spirit takes the biblical ideas that run like a spine through the dramatic story we have sought to tell here. And He makes you think subjectively about yourself. To begin praying when you're reading this book is as natural as can be.

Perhaps it has already begun. In any case, you need not stop calling upon the Lord until you are absolutely sure about Jesus Christ, until you really know that you have eternal life, until you really understand the words of John, the Apostle: "I write these things to you who believe in the name of the Son of God so that you may know that you have eternal life." (1 John 5:13).

Later you will look back and say, "Now I can really understand what happened at Toccoa Falls College. I really can."

Heaven and earth will pass away,
but my words will never pass away.

Mark 13:31

A ROBIN ON THE ROOF

Before the sun ever dawned that dark morning in November, a robin began to sing heartily on the upper reaches of LeTourneau Hall, a women's dormitory on campus. What its loss had been, no one knew. But it had a song. A blind student at Toccoa Falls College, who could not be overpowered by the sight of the devastation all around, was the one to hear the tiny bird.

But President Opperman was not there to hear it. He was hundreds of miles away in Florida and pressing hard to get back to Toccoa.

On July 4, 1976, Opperman, 52, had suffered a heart attack. Seven more attacks followed, culminating on July 13. For the following ten weeks, Kenn Opperman, the former missionary to Peru, hung on a thread between life and death.

On September 27, 1976, open-heart surgery was performed and a week later Opperman walked out of the hospital.

One of the reasons for the nearly fatal attack, he now believes, is that he wasn't entirely trusting the Lord whom he serves. The financial needs of the college and his obligation to meet a payroll month after month without resources seemed an insuperable burden.

Still he believed God would intervene in the life of Toccoa Falls College.

The Scripture to which he had clung was Psalm 66:12, "We went through fire and water, but you brought us to a place of abundance." Not until after November 6 did he really observe that water was mentioned in the text.

The weekend that the dam burst, Opperman had gone to Florida to participate in the funeral of Richele Hornbeek. Richele was a popular sophomore who had been critically injured on the way back to Toccoa Falls after a long weekend at home.

Her death, when it came, had a remarkable effect on her home church, the First Alliance of Orlando. Many of her friends were on her prayer list, which was made public at the funeral, and they were deeply moved when they discovered that they had been the subjects of Richele's prayers. The fatal accident also profoundly touched Toccoa Falls College while she lingered in a coma after the accident. Her death caused the whole college family to think about eternity very seriously. Just on the eve of November 6.

At 1:45 a.m., while the flood was still in progress, Bob Opperman's call reached his father in Florida.

He had become aware of the commotion and had reached the lower campus area in time to see the aftermath of the big wave go through. Though young Opperman thought most of the college was washing away, later it became clear that only about one-third of the campus had been affected.

Vice president Moser also called Opperman in Orlando. The college president sought assurance that order would be maintained and that no students would attempt heroics.

The 9:30 a.m. flight from Orlando to Atlanta was booked solid, but when the nature of Dr. Opperman's mission became known, the airline bumped a member of its staff to accommodate him.

Mr. J. J. Fowler, Atlanta businessman and chairman of the Board of Trustees, met Opperman in Atlanta and together they drove northeast toward Toccoa. At the outset of the journey their car radio reported eleven dead. By the time they arrived at Toccoa, the known casualties had reached thirty-three.

Because of the continuing water flow over the bridge at Route 17, the bridge was not passable and a policeman forbade Opperman to cross to Stephens County Hospital and the stricken campus on the other side.

"But I'm the college president," Opperman objected.

"You're the twelfth college president who's tried to cross here," he was told. Dr. Opperman came on across the bridge anyway.

Opperman headed for the hospital where he verified the identifications of some of the bodies. There, too, he learned that his secretary, Betty Jean Woerner, and her daughter had also died.

General Billy Jones of the U.S. Armed Forces, Civil Defense, directed procedures for handling the tragedy. Some looting had already taken place and more was feared.

The looting, though not widespread, was irritating. And it was in stark contrast to the magnificent outpouring of sympathy and help that immediately began to arrive.

The governmental assistance was instantaneous and generous.

There was an overwhelming and deep response from the citizens of Toccoa and its environs.

Georgia's Governor George Busbee remained on the campus Sunday afternoon. First Lady Rosalynn Carter, visibly moved by what she had seen, offered her help and promised to encourage the President to declare Toccoa Falls College a Federal Disaster Area.

President Carter had heard the news in the First Baptist Church in Washington and had decided during the service to ask his wife to go to Georgia. Mrs. Carter's presence on the Toccoa Falls College campus dramatically focused the attention of the world on the disaster and a battered but determined college family.

The day after the flood, the World Relief Commission of the National Association of Evangelicals presented a check for $50,000.

The Christian and Missionary Alliance pledged $25,000 and at the writing of this book had sent $42,000 to Toccoa Falls College.

Dr. Billy Graham dispatched an associate, Dr. Grady Wilson, to personally deliver $25,000, and he also sent this telegram:

Just heard of the tragedy and glory of the flood on my way to our next crusade in the Philippines. While shocked and grieving for those that lost loved ones yet thrilled at the glorious witness for Christ on the front pages of the newspapers. Have given instructions for our organization to do all in its power to be of help and am certain that God has a purpose and that His grace will be more than sufficient.

Pope Paul sent personal condolences by way of Archbishop Donellan of Atlanta. Paul was the pontiff with whom Opperman had argued years before about the persecution in South America, but in subsequent conversations their relationship had mellowed and, remarkably, in eight out of nine audiences over a span of years, Pope Paul had questioned and probed Opperman, "How do you know you have eternal life?" Repeatedly, Dr. Opperman had cited biblical passages and affirmed that for those reasons he knew he had eternal life.

And the aged Pope had not forgotten.

The Vatican's telegram read:

Holy Father grieved to learn of disaster in Toccoa causing such great loss of life and suffering. He would ask you to convey to bereaved families the expression of his sincere sympathy and his prayerful solidarity with all afflicted by the calamity.

There were other outpourings of grief. At least one hundred telegrams and letters from college presidents and student groups came in.

Several colleges offered to integrate Toccoa Falls College students into their own programs. A number of other colleges fasted and sent the money they would have spent on food.

A Mormon college, which had also gone through a dam break and a flood resulting in multiple deaths, sent expressions of concern and a substantial gift.

A Methodist college staged a variety show—and sent the proceeds.

Broadcasters also did their part. Dr. Robert H. Schuller invited Dr. Opperman to speak on his nationwide television program. He then invited his audience to send help to Toccoa Falls College. And Schuller's loyal audience did exactly that.

Pat Robertson, genial host of *The 700 Club* and the leader of the Christian Broadcasting Network, also gave Opperman an opportunity to tell the Toccoa Falls College story. Robertson himself was deeply moved by what he heard. Later his association forwarded $50,000 to the college.

The flow of monetary gifts came from all over the world and mounted at this writing to over a million dollars.

Every day the mail brought additional expressions of love and concern.

From Arizona, for example, came this letter from an Indian Mission:

The people here at Pinin Navajo Gospel Church wanted you to know that they care about you and have been praying for you . . . .

On hearing of the disaster at the Bible school, they wanted to help, so they took up this offering at a prayer meeting. One lady had no money so she put in her necklace. Maybe you can sell it and use the money . . .

A 104-year-old American woman living in England commended Toccoa on "the spunk" with which they were facing the tragedy and sent $2,000.

A man from Pennsylvania wrote:

I was very sorry to hear about your disaster with the flooding. In a way I praise God for it though. Let me explain why. On the news I saw how your people at the college were still praising and loving God. I gave my life to Jesus during that newscast, and I now have Jesus in my heart . . . .

Another man wrote, "My wife and I were converted yesterday. I have just realized that God has been blessing me all my life and I have a lot of catching up to do." He included a gift for the college.

A pastor from Florida wrote that he had sought a word from the Lord concerning what had taken place. The answer he received was Psalm 46:5: "God is in the midst of her; she will not be moved: God will help her when morning dawns."

Many of the letters contained checks to help restore the beautiful campus and meet other pressing needs.

A pastor in South Carolina, for example, approached several manufacturers for help and support. In all he raised about $8,000 plus a quantity of goods—including twelve cases of diapers!

One of the letters that President Opperman remembered most fondly came at a time when he especially needed a lift. This letter from a Roman Catholic priest provided encouragement and a laugh too: "Time will go by and people will have forgotten something. So here's $100 to buy grass seed."

One woman said, "Here's the widow's mite. This is all I've got."

Yet another woman sent the money she had saved for her husband's Christmas gift. She explained, "My husband wanted to help Toccoa Falls more than anything else in his life. When you accept this gift you will give him the desires of his heart."

We could continue—for the letters, telegrams, and offers of help went on and on. And so did the love and concern expressed toward Toccoa Falls College.

Total damage to the campus and its residents, along with restoration and recovery costs, were estimated at more than six million dollars. The first $450,000 that was received included all insurance claims and many gifts and was dispersed to students and others who suffered personal loss.

Only when that need was met were funds applied to the recovery of the College.

Opperman did not follow a policy any different from Presidents Bandy and Forrest before him. The College simply trusted in God.

As has always happened in the past, they believed at Toccoa Falls College that God would provide. He would motivate people to give gifts and God's work would go on.

They knew it.

And my God will meet all your needs
according to his glorious riches in Christ Jesus.

PHILIPPIANS 4:19

CHAPTER 24

AND SINCE THE FLOOD

Many years have passed since the flood.

Direct evidences of the damage are no more. Instead, on every side there is evidence of vigor and life. The Falls themselves are strikingly beautiful and continue to attract thousands of visitors each year. There are many new buildings and renovations to enhance the updated campus.

Dam Break in Georgia, the book in your hand, has been sold and given away in large numbers. More than 100,000 copies were sold immediately after the flood. In the years since, another 200,000 copies have been distributed, 20,000 of them inside the prisons of America.

In the decades since this story was recounted, many more dramatic stories have been reported as a result of people reading the book, which continues to bless readers and gives glory to God.

Not long after the flood, a Christian truck driver pulled into a truck-stop restaurant. Seeing a depressed-looking man sitting in a corner, he approached him. Could they talk, he wanted to know. The answer was a sharp rebuff. However, the impression persisted until finally the truck driver approached the man again. "Listen, I am a Christian and I am supposed to talk to you." It turned out that the man was a new believer, a salesman. He had just phoned home, only to hear an unexpected voice on the other end of the line informing him that his wife and two small children had been killed in an automobile accident. He had been sitting there trying to summon the courage to go home and face his own appalling personal disaster.

The truck driver hurried to his rig for a copy of *Dam Break in Georgia*, and gave it to the distraught husband and father. Plunging in immediately, the devastated man read it all the way through. And early in the morning he headed for the truck driver's motel room. He was ready now, he said, to face the heartbreak at home. Strength and courage had come to one more person through the compelling accounts of the survivors of the flood at Toccoa Falls College.

The saga continues through the life of a college that has experienced both fire and flood—and a great deal of pain. The ministry also continues through the lives of those who survived the waters to emerge into an enlarging morning of joy.

Through it all, the Scripture that has been so meaningful in the life of the College still stands: *"We went through fire and water, but you brought us to a place of abundance"* (Psalm 66:12).

AFTERWORD

In 1919, four years after a fire nearly destroyed Toccoa Falls Institute, Paul Rader penned the words of the well-known hymn, "Only Believe." As he stood looking over the campus, the faith and courage of the students and faculty moved Rader. The last stanza of the hymn affirms God's presence in darkness and dawn.

Fear not, precious flock, from the cross to the throne
From death into life He went for His own
All power in earth, all power above
Is given to Him for the flock of His love

Fear not, precious flock, He goeth ahead,
Your Shepherd selects the path you must tread;
The waters of Mara He'll sweeten for thee
He drank all the bitter in Gethsemane

Fear not, precious flock, whatever your lot;
He enters all rooms, the doors being shut.
He never forsakes, He never is gone,
So count on His presence in darkness and dawn.

REFRAIN:
Only believe, only believe;
All things are possible, only believe;

Only believe, only believe;
All things are possible, only believe.

"Only Believe" Author: Paul Rader© Public Domain

More than 60 years later, that same faith and courage was seen again in the lives of those affected by the devastating flood which swept through the campus. The truth of God's presence in those dark hours, the truth that God was in control, carried many through those difficult days.

This is a record of God's faithfulness, in darkness and in dawn. This is a testimony of people's responses to tragedy. "How can I help?" was a question asked over and over. Their spontaneous responses to open their homes and their hearts to the needs of those at Toccoa Falls blessed and humbled the recipients deeply.

The fact that God was in control over all of the events was clear. To hold back the waters would have been no great thing for so great a God. In allowing the waters to be released, His greatness was revealed through the faithfulness and testimonies of His children. As one survivor explained, "We know that God was with us through the flood. He was with those who escaped. He was with the 39 people who died. Because of the flood, we know that God will be with us through anything we ever have to face."

In all things, to God be the glory.

IN MEMORIAM

Richele Marie Hornbeek

Karen Anderson
Joseph Anderson
Rebecca Anderson
Gerald Brittin
William L. Ehrensberger
Peggy Ann Ehrensberger
Robert Ehrensberger
Kristen Ehrensberger
Kenny Ehrensberger
David Fledderjohann
Mary Jo Ginther
Brenda Ginther
Rhonda Ginther
Nancy Ginther
Tracy Ginther
Cary E. Hanna
Tiep Harner
Robbie Harner
Christopher Kemp
Cassandra Metzger
Dirksen Metzger

Ruth Moore
Jeremiah Moore
Edward E. Pepsny
Carol Pepsny
Paul Pepsny
Bonnie Pepsny
Eloise J. Pinney
Monroe J. Rupp
Jerry Sproull
Melissa Sproull
Jocelyn Sproull
Joanna Sproull
Richard J. Swires
Jaimée Veer
Mary N. Williams
Paul I. Williams
Betty Jean Woerner
Deborah Woerner

Bertha Walls

APPENDIX A

A CHRONOLOGY OF EVENTS

The following timeline gives an approximate account by eyewitnesses of the horrifying events that took place early Sunday morning, November 6, 1977.

Saturday, November 5, 1977

9:00 p.m. — Members of the Toccoa Falls Volunteer Fire Department were already concerned about the rising waters of Toccoa Creek due to the amount of rain that had fallen.

10:30 p.m. — Ron Ginther and David Fledderjohann took the Toccoa Falls Volunteer Fire Department truck up to the dam and visually inspected the water level. The water in the dam appeared to be below danger level and there was no water running down the road. They radioed back by CB that the dam was solid and there appeared to be no need for concern or alarm.

11:30 p.m. — David Fledderjohann went home to spend an hour with his wife before being called out again. Mrs. Decie Fowler, mother-in-law of Roy Gaines, the mayor of Toccoa, had just died. Drivers of the hearse from the funeral home in Royston had come to pick up her body and were among the last known to drive across the Toccoa Creek before the dam broke.

Sunday, November 6, 1977

12:15 a.m.— Security guard Jim Conaway called Eldon Elsberry concerned about the rising water. By this time, others of the Volunteer Fire Department had gathered.

1:10 a.m.—Volunteer firemen left Ron Ginther's trailer where they had enjoyed a short break with coffee and cookies. Fledderjohann and volunteer firemen headed to Sproull's house to warn them of flooding.

1:20 a.m. — Dee Pinney left the Ginther's trailer, where he had been working on a CB, and headed toward upper campus. When he got to the bridge near Trailerville, the lights went out on lower campus.

1:25 a.m. — The water pressure behind the dam became an irresistible force, and a torrent of water surged toward the lip of Toccoa Falls. As Pinney neared Forrest Hall, he could see turbulent water ahead on the road near Gate Cottage. Backing up, he tried to turn around to warn people that the dam had broken. With water up to the floorboard of the car and no longer able to see the road, Pinney left his vehicle and headed for the hill below Stewart Hall. At the same time, Greg Bandy, grandson of the former president of the college, hearing the roar of rushing water, looked out his window from his grandparents' house. The Bandy House stood about 30 feet above the creek, and he could not even see Forrest Hall across the creek.

1:35 a.m. — The old school bell on campus was rung to give warning, since the electricity was out and there was no other way to signify an alarm. Dee Pinney made his way to the fire hall and drove the fire truck to the hospital, sounding the siren as he went. At the hospital, Pinney called the Toccoa Fire Department and told them that the dam had broken at Toccoa Falls. Shortly after, volunteer fireman Eldon Elsberry, covered with mud, joined Pinney at the hospital.

1:40 a.m. — Emergency medical technicians with the Stephens County Hospital were contacted by radio in the ambulance reporting that the dam had broken. Shortly after, Toccoa police arrived at the Highway 17 bridge where EMTs had already pulled a woman out of the water.

1:45 a.m. — The dispatcher at the Stephens County jail was notified of the flood. The dispatcher radioed the information to patrolling deputies and called Sheriff Don Shirley at his home. Fred Purdy, Toccoa-Stephens County Civil Defense Director, received a call from the Toccoa Police Department about the dam break at Toccoa Falls.

2:00 a.m. — Civil Defense Unit leaders and volunteer rescue workers were at the bridge.

2:30 a.m. — Groups of volunteers from neighboring Georgia counties began arriving at the bridge to give assistance. The Toccoa rescue squad had been joined by the Toccoa Civil Air Patrol and members of the local Civil Defense office.

3:00 a.m. — The Salvation Army moved in with supplies of coffee, food, and aid for victims and searchers, followed soon after by the Red Cross. Several private contractors volunteered heavy machinery and personnel to begin clearing debris. Greg Bandy and other searchers entered Forrest Hall and discovered one of the first victims of the flood.

4:00 a.m. — The process of moving survivors out of the area had almost been completed. By daylight literally the whole world had heard about the disaster at Toccoa Falls through news broadcasts. Unceasing offers of help began to pour in from all over as the search for the missing continued. Original reports of 10 dead swelled first to 15, then to 20, and still counting.

Throughout the day — For years, Stephens County rescue agencies had coordinated rescue drills with the hospital, using Toccoa Falls College students as the victims. Now it was for real. Their drills paid off. Later they were commended for their thoroughness and for how smoothly and quickly they had acted.

Mid-Morning — Governor George Busbee, dressed in Army fatigues, toured the devastation, along with an army of reporters from all over the nation. The governor officially declared Toccoa to be in a state of emergency. In Washington, D.C., First Lady Rosalynn Carter made preparation to fly to Toccoa for a tour and to meet survivors.

Noon — Rescue workers had compiled an accurate list of the dead and missing.

3:00 p.m. — Mrs. Carter arrived to tour the disaster area and visit with survivors in the hospital and on campus.

4:00 p.m. — Students met with college president Dr. Kenn Opperman who told them the school would be closed until November 15. Many residents were housed at the Georgia Baptist Assembly Conference Center, some were taken in by residents of Toccoa, and others joined their families for the interim.

5:30 p.m. — The last of 38 bodies was found. The body of the 39th victim, "Uncle" Paul Williams, would not be discovered downstream until nearly a month later.

Monday, November 7, 1977

President Jimmy Carter declared Toccoa Falls College a national disaster area.

Wednesday, November 16, 1977

8:00 a.m. — A heavy shower preceded an early morning memorial service held in the Student Center, marking the resuming of operations at Toccoa Falls College. As 1,500 participants arrived that morning, they beheld a magnificent double rainbow stretched over campus. It seemed to symbolize God's blessing and a promise that Toccoa Falls College would survive.

A Year Later

"None of us here at Toccoa Falls College will ever be able to forget the havoc and loss of November 6, 1977, nor will we be able to forget the way in which people pitched in to help. We have no idea how many people helped, but we do know that hundreds of volunteers worked rescuing the injured and recovering the bodies. Many more helped clear the rubble. More than 1,700 churches, 5,000 individuals, 90 colleges, and hundreds of manufacturers and merchants sent help. Fifty private and public agencies worked around the clock in the recovery." ("A Cup of Cold Water," by Dr. James Grant. *TFC Today,* Vol. 3, No. 2, 1978.)

APPENDIX B

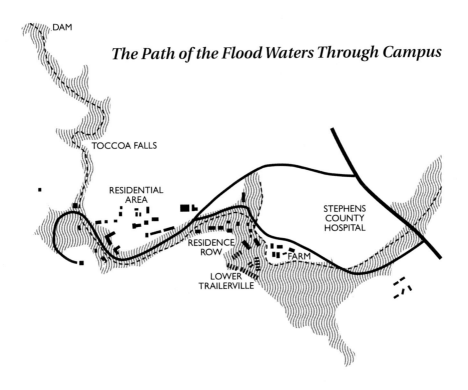

The Path of the Flood Waters Through Campus

DAM

TOCCOA FALLS

RESIDENTIAL AREA

STEPHENS COUNTY HOSPITAL

RESIDENCE ROW

FARM

LOWER TRAILERVILLE

ABOUT THE AUTHORS

K. Neill Foster, Ph. D., has authored and co-authored numerous books and academic articles.

Eric Mills was Book Editor with Horizon House Publishers.

CREDITS

Map and timeline of events: *Brenda Ritchey*

Photos: *Paul M. Brown, Kelly Vickers, Clarence Zeches, The Toccoa Record, Toccoa Falls College Archives*

Design and typesetting: *Beth VanDyke*

First and Second Edition written materials: *Bea Rupp, Ken Sanders*

Third Edition additional written materials: *Angela Ramage, Brenda Ritchey*

Third Edition editing: *Kelly Vickers*

For additional copies of *Dam Break in Georgia*, contact Toccoa Falls Books and Gifts at (706) 886-6831, ext. 5257.